CAPE ②
AMERICA

⑥ JOHN CHEEVER The Journals ⑩ RUSSELL HOBAN I, that was a child, my tongue's use sleeping ⑮ HAROLD BRODKEY The River ⑲ DAVID RIEFF Los Angeles: Capital of the Third World *with photographs by* ANTHONY HERNANDEZ ㉖ WHITNEY BALLIETT Jazz Funerals *with photographs by* LEE FRIEDLANDER ㉟ BETH NUGENT City of Boys ㊷ MICHAEL ORMEROD Photographs ㊹ BOHUMIL HRABAL The White Horse ■

㊾ *Contributors*

THE JOURNALS
C*John* HE

John CHEEVER

Photograph by Michael Ormerod

WHEN JOHN CHEEVER DIED IN 1982, HE LEFT BEHIND TWENTY-NINE LOOSELEAF NOTEBOOKS – HIS JOURNALS – BEGUN IN THE LATE 1940S AND CONTINUED THROUGH MORE THAN THREE DECADES. HIS COMMITMENT TO THEM WAS OF CENTRAL IMPORTANCE TO HIS LIFE.
THIS EXTRACT IS TAKEN FROM 1952.

In middle age there is mystery, there is mystification. The most I can make out of this hour is a kind of loneliness. Even the beauty of the visible world seems to crumble, yes even love. I feel that there has been some miscarriage, some wrong turning, but I do not know when it took place and I have no hope of finding it.

Thinking for a week about Leander, Betsey, and Eben without writing a word, without making any progress. And so I see all my plans – the voyage to Genoa, etc. – collapse. Is there something intrinsically wrong with these three, that I can't grasp them? Thinking this morning to discard the opera.

Yesterday was rainy and deeply overcast. At four B. and I walked up Holbrook Road to the K.s'. The clearing wind had begun to blow. As the overcast was displaced with brilliance and color, as more and more light poured into the valley, the hour seemed tumultuous and exalting. Backgammon and gin.

Skating one afternoon at the Newberrys'. The end of a very cold winter day. The ice, contracting in the cold, made a noise like thunder. Walking up the frozen field to the house we could hear it thundering. We went back that night. There was no one else on the pond. The Granowski's dog was barking. There was no moon and the ice was black. It seemed, skating out into the center of the pond, that the number of stars I could see was multiplied. They seemed as thickly sown as a rush of snowflakes. As I skated back to the end of the pond, the number seemed to diminish. I was confounded. It could have been the whiskey and the wine. It could have been my utter ignorance of cosmology.

To church; the second Sunday in Lent. From the bank president's wife behind me drifted the smell of camphor from her furs, and the stales of her breath, as she sang, 'Glory be to the Father, and to the Son, and to the Holy Ghost; As it was in the beginning, is now, and ever shall be, world without end.' The Old Testament dealt with should the Father eat bitter grapes; the New with an eye for an eye and a tooth for a tooth. The sermon with the doctrine of Incantation. The rector has a plain mind. If it has any charms, they are the charms of plainness. Through inheritance and cultivation he has reached an impermeable homeliness. His mind and his face are one. He spoke of the impressive historical documentation of Christ's birth, miracles, and death. The church is meant to evoke rural England. The summoning bells, the late-winter sunlight, the lancet windows, the hand-cut stone. But these are real fragments of a real past. World without end, I murmur, shutting my eyes, Amen.

But I seem to stand outside the realm of God's mercy.

I would like not to be vindictive or narrow. I would like to avoid phony compassion. Thinking of the midsummer night, '*Parlons français*,' the drunkard said. I see that this is small. I see in the five-and-ten-cent store yesterday that my descriptions of Betsey's pleasure are small. It stinks of peanuts and cheap candy. A love song drifts over from the phonograph-record department. The salesgirl is elaborately painted. You buy what you want; and you leave. The street is sunny. The blind Negress on the bus says, 'I'm by myself. I'm by myself at home now. I'm by myself on the street. I'm by myself. I'm by myself so much I'm like a statue. I'm by myself like a statue all the time.' She shakes her portable radio. 'She ain't working. I've had her on since Ninety-sixth Street and she ain't made a sound. I guess I'll have to get her fixed again. She wears out quick.' The man on the train. '*Well*, I guess I look cheerful enough, but I'm on my way to the hospital. They just called me from the office to tell me that C. fell out of an apple tree and broke her leg in two places. They called me at the office a few minutes ago and I rushed over here and took the train . . . '

These Westchester Sunday nights. There has usually been a party on Saturday night so you wake up with a faint hangover and a mouth burned by a green cigar. The clothes you have left in a heap on the floor smell of stale perfume. You take a shower. You put on old clothes. You drive your wife to church and your children to Sunday school. You rake the leaves off the flower bed. They are too wet to burn. You put a chemical fertilizer on the lawn and examine the bulbs. The Rockinhams, on their way to a Sunday-lunch party at the Armstrongs', shout their good mornings from the sidewalk. 'Isn't it a glorious day; glorious, glorious.' Your wife and children return from church, still in their stiff clothes. You have a drink before lunch. Sometimes there are guests. You take a walk; you rake more leaves. The children scatter to play with other children. The southbound local, the train that aunts, uncles, and cousins who have gone into the suburbs for lunch take home; the train that cooks, maids, butlers, and other menservants take into town for their half holiday. Sunday is almost over.

Awake before dawn, feeling tired and full of resolutions. Do not drink. Do not et cetera, et cetera. The noise of birdsong swelling: flickers, chickadees, cardinals. Then in the midst of this loud noise I thought I heard a parrot. 'Prolly want a crackeer,' he said. 'Prolly want a crackeer.' Woke tired and took the 7:44. The river blanketed with a mist. The voices overheard. 'Well, then she boiled it and then she broiled it.' He raised his face and drew over it a beatific look as if he were tasting last night's dinner again. 'Well, we've got one of those electric rotisseries.' 'Oh, New York's nothing like Chicago; nothing like it.' On Twenty-third Street I read a sign: 'DON'T LOSE YOUR LOVED ONE BECAUSE OF UGLY FAT.' There was a window full of crucifixes made out of plastic. The surface of the city is paradoxical. For a mind cast in paradox it is reassuring to find this surface. Thinking again, in the dentist's chair, that I am like a prisoner who is trying to escape from jail by the wrong route.

EVER

For all one knows, that door may stand open, although I continue to dig a tunnel with a teaspoon. Oh, I think, if I could only taste a little success. But don't I approach it by deepening the pit in which I stand? Mary in the morning, asleep, looking like the girl I fell in love with. Her round arms lie outside the covers. Her brown hair is loose. The abiding quality of seriousness and pureness.

In the dark hour you cannot call on goods and chattels to save you, or old ski trails or the paths to streams. You must find something greater. And the mind in which the forces of contumely and destruction seem greater than the forces of creativity. Creativity is there, but it seems, in relation to the forces of destruction, like the nipple on a balloon. So, made up of so much destruction and with such a slender knowledge of love he appears poorly as a husband, and lover – masked in a rag of a smile and a striped tie and a few faint observations. Oh so deeply rooted in this mind are the needs and the habits of prayer. Having triumphantly separated himself from the foolishness of religion, he goes by the church – he hears the bells in the morning – in the churlish and unhappy frame of mind of a man who has been excommunicated. He feels the lash of expulsion. And oh this poor mind, casting desperately around a room for some detail that will give it form and meaning, seizes always on an ashtray heaped with butts or a crooked stocking, a tear in the rug. And then he sees the sky! the poignant blue, the line of darkness rising like a lid; the perfect clearness of line and color that means that a northwest wind has scoured the overcast and blown it out to sea. So his mind wanders between the ashtray and the twilight while most of the known world lies somewhere in between. He worries, he worries about his mustache, his old navy raincoat, his weight, his hair, his teeth, the stiffness in his left knee, and if his anxiety ever transcends this it is to worry about a nation of paltry men, conceived in his image and likeness – or, if he is a world federalist, to worry about a world. Why has the sweetness gone? It would all come back with a new car or a bonus or a little of the recognition that he deserves for his hard work. A convertible; a trip to Spain.

The stubborn dreariness of this rainy Sunday. Down at the station there are only a few travellers for the southbound local. A cook with a paper bag full of leftovers and a hand-me-down coat is going to Yonkers to visit her relations. A maiden aunt out for Sunday lunch is returning. The last is a figure of mystery, a man in a worn polo coat beneath which show the striped pants and boiled shirt of a tuxedo. These are the only passengers and they seem to have come here unwilling to catch a train and make a hopeless journey. In the waiting room and the cabstand, both of them unattended, a telephone rings and rings and rings. Fishnets for shad and bass are strung out into the water, and the rain, like a much finer net, encircles the country with a stir of reassuring and dreary noise. Racks of string hang above the railroad track like the old-fashioned fly nets worn by livery horses. It is a stubborn and an infinite dreariness, rooted in the stupor, the discomfort, or the downright misery of a heavy churchgoer's lunch. The ballgame has been rained out but not the 'Emperor' Concerto or the 'Jupiter' Symphony. More than half the world is in an unrefreshing sleep.

But between the waiting room and the freight house there is a view of water and mountains. The eye goes up for miles and miles, for while the little rain makes the shore dim, nothing is obscured. Here there is more power and space than you had expected. The smudge from a distant tugboat, discouraged and scattered by the little rain, drifts toward the water. There is a mountain as round as a plump knee and a mountain cut like a cock's crest and even a faint smell of the wilderness – dead bloodworms and wet corduroy – for three fishermen are strung along the narrow bank between the railroad tracks and the water. Oh it is so dreary that one's teeth seem literally to ache. The smell of boiled beef lingers in the upstairs hall.

As I approach my fortieth birthday without having accomplished any one of the things I intended to accomplish – without even having achieved the deep creativity that I have worked for all this time – I feel that I take a minor, an obscure, a dim position that is not my destiny but that is my fault, as if I had lacked, somewhere along the line, the wit and courage to contain myself competently within the shapes at hand. I think of Leander and all the others. It is not that these are stories of failure; that is not what is frightening. It is that they are dull annals; that they are of no import; that Leander, walking in the garden at dusk in the throes of a violent passion, is of no importance to anyone. It does not matter . . .

In town for lunch. The air-conditioning, the smell of perfume and gin, the attentions of the headwaiter, the real and unreal sense of haste, importance, and freedom that clings to the theatre. It was a beautiful day in town, windy, clear, and fresh. The girls on the street are a joy. A girl with bare shoulders on Fifty-seventh Street; dark eyes and light eyes and red hair and above all the wonderful sense of dignity and purpose in their clear features. But there is the imperfect joining of the carnal world and the world of courage and other spiritual matters. I seem, after half a lifetime, to have made no progress, unless resignation is progress. There is the erotic hour of waking, which is like birth. There is the light or the rainfall, some ingenuous symbol by which one returns to the visible, perhaps the mature world. There is the euphoria, the sense that life is no more than it appears to be, light and water and trees and pleasant people that can be brought crashing down by a neck, a hand, an obscenity written on a toilet door. There is always, somewhere, this hint of aberrant carnality. The worst of it is that it seems labyrinthine; I come back again and again to the image of a naked prisoner in an unlocked cell, and to tell the truth I don't know how he will escape. Death figures here, the unwillingness to live. Many of these shapes seem like the shapes of death; one approaches them with the same amorousness, the same sense of terrible dread. I say to myself that the body can be washed clean of any indulgence; the only sin is despair, but I speak meaninglessly in my own case. Chasteness is real; the morning adjures one to be chaste. Chasteness is waking. I could not wash the obscenity off myself. But in all this thinking there is a lack of space, of latitude, of light and humor. Thinking back to 'The Reasonable Music', it seems to me, for this reason, to be a bad, a febrile, story. Play a little baseball and the Gordian knot crumbles into dust.

Is there anything more wonderful than the Monday morning train: the 8:22? The weekend – say a long weekend like the Fourth – has left you rested. There have been picnics, fireworks, excursions to the beach – all the pleasant things we do together. On Sunday we had cocktails late and a pickup supper in the garden. We see the darkness end the weekend without any regret – it has all been so pleasant. In the garden we can hear, from the west, the noise of traffic on the parkway rise to a high pitch that it will hold until nearly midnight, as other families drive back to the city from the mountains or the shore; and the sleeping children, the clothing hung in the back seat, the infinity of headlights – the sense we take from these overcrowded Sunday roads of a gigantic pilgrimage – is all a part of this hour. You water the grass, tell the children a story, take a bath, and get into bed. The morning is brilliant and fresh. Your wife drives you to the train in the convertible. The children and the dog come along. From the minute you wake up you seem to be on the verge of an irrepressible joy. The drive down Alewives Lane to the station seems triumphal, and when you see the station below you and the trees and the few people who have already gathered there, waiting in the morning sun, and when you kiss your wife and your children goodbye and give the dog's ears a scratch and say good morning all around the platform and unfold the *Tribune* and hear the train, the 8:22, coming down the tracks, it seems to me a wonderful thing.

© Mary Cheever, Susan Cheever, Benjamin Cheever, and Federico Cheever, 1991

'TO DISGUISE NOTHING, TO CONCEAL NOTHING, TO WRITE ABOUT THOSE THINGS THAT ARE CLOSEST TO OUR PAIN, OUR HAPPINESS; TO WRITE ABOUT MY SEXUAL CLUMSINESS, THE AGONIES OF TANTALUS, THE DEPTH OF MY DISCOURAGEMENT – I SEEM TO GLIMPSE IT IN MY DREAMS – MY DESPAIR. TO WRITE ABOUT THE FOOLISH AGONIES OF ANXIETY, THE REFRESHMENT OF OUR STRENGTH WHEN THESE ARE ENDED; TO WRITE ABOUT OUR PAINFUL SEARCH FOR SELF, JEOPARDIZED BY A STRANGER IN THE POST OFFICE, A HALF-SEEN FACE IN A TRAIN WINDOW; TO WRITE ABOUT THE CONTINENTS AND POPULATIONS OF OUR DREAMS, ABOUT LOVE AND DEATH, GOOD AND EVIL, THE END OF THE WORLD.'

RUSSELL HOBAN

I, that was a child, my tongue's use sleeping

PHOTOGRAPH BY MICHAEL ORMEROD

EVERYONE LIVES A LIFE THAT IS SEEN AND A LIFE THAT IS UNSEEN. OUR DREAMS ARE PART OF OUR UNSEEN LIFE. We often forget our own dreams and we have no idea whatever of the dreams of others: last night the person next to you in the Underground may have ridden naked on a lion or travelled under the sea to the lost city of Atlantis. Along with the dream life there is the life of ideas and half-ideas, of glimmerings and flashes and indescribable atmospheres of the mind. What we actually do in what is called the real world depends largely on how we live this unseen life in our inner world of words and images, songs and bits of poems, names and numbers and memories and dreams remembered and unremembered. Whether the song in our heads is Michael Jackson or Franz Schubert it is fitting itself to and reinforcing something in us that comes forward to meet it. That's how art affects life; we use it to be more what we are and to become what is in us wanting us to become it. The world of the song or the poem is met by other worlds known to us or hidden in our dreams.

In dreams one often sees the house of one's childhood. Years and years have passed, one's own children have grown up and gone out into the world; but in dreams the house of childhood is fresh and strong, the smell of its closets, the creak of its floors, the light through its windows and the shadows of leaves — everything resonates in the sleeping mind. Perhaps tonight one will find the lost toy or see more clearly something only half-glimpsed long ago. And perhaps today if I begin with the house of my childhood I can find my way to that unseen part of my life that grows out of and into what is called The American Dream.

The house of my childhood was in Lansdale, Pennsylvania. My parents were Russian Jews from a town in the Ukraine called Ostrog. They're both dead now and my two sisters and I continue their outward journey from that town we've never seen. They were both young when they came to America. My father had been poor in Russia, he told me how once outside a bakery he had seen a boy with a freshly-bought cheese pastry take out the cheese and throw away the crust which he, my father, then picked up and ate. There was in our house a halting little oil painting he had done on a wooden panel: it was a platoon of Russian cavalry, horsemen with slung carbines and bedrolls, just a little clump of figures on horses, seen from the back. Now I call to mind this picture that I haven't seen for almost fifty years and I have no idea what it was to him.

My mother came to America before my father, in 1911 I think, when she was seventeen. She came with her sisters and she worked as a seamstress to earn my father's passage. He became a newsboy in Philadelphia, he had a dog who sat on the back of his bicycle. He made friends with some of the staff of the *Jewish Daily Forward* who used to buy papers from him. He went to night classes and lectures; I am named after Dr Russell Conwell who gave a famous lecture called 'Acres of Diamonds' in which a man travelled the world in search of wealth and then found it in his own backyard.

My father bought Dr Eliot's Five-Foot Shelf, the Harvard Classics; also E. Haldeman-Julius's Little Blue Books in one of which Dr Emil Coué said that every day in every way he was getting better and better; also Krafft-Ebing's *Psychopathia Sexualis* in which all the best parts were in Latin; also *Sunshine and Health Magazine* in which respectable ladies and gentlemen were shown in respectably drooping nakedness drinking tea and playing tennis.

My father gave me a book, *Fairy Tales for Worker's Children*. I was taught never to cross a picket line and always to eat the union label on loaves of rye and pumpernickel for good luck. My father had become Advertising Manager of the *Jewish Daily Forward* and Director of the Drama Guild of the Labor Institute of the Workmen's Circle of Philadelphia. He directed Yiddish classics and contemporary American plays of social comment such as *Stevedore, 1931*, and *Can You Hear Their Voices?* Sometimes my sisters and I got onstage; in the play *1931* a jobless man begged a dime from a passerby who tossed it so that it fell to the ground. I was a newsboy who grabbed the dime. I had one line to speak: 'It's mine, I saw it first!'

My mother raised pigeons, two thousand of them. We had a hired nan who helped with the pigeons and our one-acre truck patch. My father's younger brother, my uncle Jack, had a frequently brokendown roadster called Natasha and liked to play baseball. Sometimes I rode in Natasha's rumble seat. On the wall by my bed I had a chromolithographed cardboard display figure of King Kong on top of the Empire State Building with an airplane in one hand and Fay Wray in the other. Ethel Waters sang 'Stormy Weather' on the radio and sad-faced men came to the back door and asked if they could do some chores for a meal. My mother fed them and I sat on the porch with them while they ate their share of the American Dream.

One speaks of the American Dream and the meaning varies with the speaker but always what is meant is a montage of heart-pictures, desire-pictures, richly coloured wishes and memories and expectations of what people variously want from America or associate with America. This montage may have in it the Declaration of Independence, John D. Rockefeller, the Ku Klux Klan, Daniel Boone and Joseph McCarthy, Shirley Temple and the mountain men and Charlie Parker; it may have Abe Lincoln and Billy the Kid and the Statue of Liberty lifting her lamp beside the golden door of the Land of Opportunity where the plough breaks the plains, the West is won, the Yanks are coming, the Wright brothers and the astronauts go up and the economy comes down, Henry David Thoreau plants beans at Walden Pond, the Okies roll out of the dustbowl in battered Fords and talking blues by Woody Guthrie, Frank Sinatra sings at Las Vegas, Thomas Wolfe burns in the night and Jack Dempsey, Marilyn Monroe, Diamond Jim Brady, P. T. Barnum and the *Enola Gay* gleam in the high sunlight over Hiroshima while Bartolomeo Vanzetti writes a letter to his son and survivalists in Texas stockpile provisions and machine guns. The American Dream is pretty much whatever montage of heart-pictures you like to look at.

In every montage of heart-pictures lives the house of childhood, the physical one that still stands and perhaps is lived in by strangers or has burnt down or been demolished or stands desolate with broken suitcases and old letters with blurred writing under rotting leaves and broken glass and the rain coming in through empty windows.

There is another house of childhood and this one is of the mind. In my house of childhood of the mind lives Vol XVII. of the Harvard Classics. Vol. XVII was the only book in the Five-Foot Shelf much handled; Locke and Hume and Darwin looked as new as the day they were unpacked but Vol. XVII was *Folklore and Fable*, Andersen and Aesop and the brothers Grimm, and it was in heavy use. Oscar Wilde's *House of Pomegranates* and *The Arabian Nights* live there also. As a child I did much of my reading in the room in our house called the library. It was lined with books in Russian, Yiddish, and English and had a massive oak table. No one else I knew had such a room. I had outdoor reading places as well, and of these my favourite was a big old wild cherry tree where in season I read *Robin Hood* and ate little sun-warmed black cherries.

This house that childhood builds in the mind is a learning place and a place where we test words and images and ideas to find out what rings true. Also it's like a safe house in a spy film: in it the secret agent that is the child's mind can stay hidden until ready to venture armed into the hostile city. It isn't the world that is hostile – the stone and the leaf and the door of the world beckon and welcome – it's the grey city of the world that threatens, the grey city of the failed children of the world, the dry thinkers, the juiceless minds, the poison skulls that dream in numbers and megadeaths. They run the world, these failed children; they speak in all languages and in all languages their speech is vile. In bemedalled uniforms, in costly business suits and ties they mouth pompous words printed out by grey machines. Each one thinks the other is the enemy while the real enemy, the monster they have called up together, sings to itself outside the window. The grey city is why the safe house of childhood of the mind is needed, and long after the child is grown this safe house is still needed in the shadows and the narrow alleys by the waterfront in the grey city of terror.

This house of childhood is not a foolish place, it is the true place where first recognitions happen all through life; it is the place where I heard for the first time what is in the Beethoven quartets and Bach's *Art of Fugue* and Schubert's *Die Winterreise*; it is where Oedipus made his tragedy belong to him and was no longer a victim, where Conrad's Jim jumped from the *Patna* into lostness, where Rubashov in *Darkness at Noon* accepted one by one the consequences of the ideas he had lived by; it is where I took in unknown pages that came alive years later like water in the desert, it is where T.S. Eliot said, in *Little Gidding*:

> We die with the dying:
> See, they depart, and we go with them.
> We are born with the dead:
> See, they return, and bring us with them.
> The moment of the rose and the moment of the yew-tree
> Are of equal duration.

For the last twenty-two years I've lived in London. I'm a stranger at home under grey English skies and walking by European rivers but I still weapon and provision myself in the house of childhood that was built in America. Are there in that house recognitions that are peculiarly American? Yes, I think so. Here is one:

> Out of the cradle endlessly rocking,
> Out of the mocking-bird's throat, the musical shuttle,
> Out of the Ninth-month midnight,
> Over the sterile sands and the fields beyond, where the child leaving
>   his bed wander'd alone, bareheaded, barefoot,
> Down from the shower'd halo,
> Up from the mystic play of shadows twining and twisting
>   as if they were alive,
> Out from the patches of briers and blackberries,
> From the memories of the bird that chanted to me,
> From your memories sad brother, from the fitful risings and
>   fallings I heard,
> From under that yellow half-moon late-risen and swollen as
>   if with tears . . .

In Walt Whitman's magical lyric the poet listens through the night to the 'lone singer wonderful', the mocking-bird, the solitary he-bird who guards the nest and the eggs to which his mate never returns:

> Demon or bird! (said the boy's soul),
>   Is it indeed toward your mate you sing? or is it really to me?
> For I, that was a child, my tongue's use sleeping,
>   now I have heard you,
> Now in a moment I know what I am for, I awake,
> And already a thousand singers, a thousand songs, clearer,
>   louder and more sorrowful than yours,
> A thousand warbling echoes have started to life within me,
>   never to die.

In the last part of the poem he asks for a word from the sea:

> Whereto answering, the sea,
> Delaying not, hurrying not,
> Whisper'd me through the night, and very plainly before daybreak,
> Lisp'd to me the low and delicious word death,
> And again death, death, death, death,
> Hissing melodious, neither like the bird nor like my arous'd
>   child's heart,
> But edging near as privately for me rustling at my feet,
> Creeping thence steadily up to my ears and laving me softly all over,
> Death, death, death, death, death.
>
> Which I do not forget,
> But fuse the song of my dusky demon and brother,
> That he sang to me in the moonlight on Paumanok's gray beach,
> With the thousand responsive songs at random,
> My own songs awaked from that hour,
> And with them the key, the word up from the waves,
> The word of the sweetest song and all songs,
> That strong and delicious word which, creeping to my feet,
> (Or like some old crone rocking the cradle, swathed in
>   sweet garments, bending aside),
> The sea whisper'd me.

This poem was first published in 1859, one hundred and thirty-two years ago. At this distance Whitman seems not so much a man as a manifestation, as if the nature of America and its history generated this voice that must inevitably appear. He seems a kind of lesson, a paradigm, this Walt Whitman who read almost inaudibly to a baffled and not very responsive audience and then wrote the newspaper account of the same reading in which he described himself as filling the auditorium with his booming masculine voice and being interrupted continually by applause; Walt Whitman the non-boomer, the whisperer in the darkness at the heart of the American Dream, driven by his demon to step out from behind his laborious persona for this profound and shadowy rite of passage. Nations have national characteristics: I think that we Americans have both a propensity for bullshit and an inborn drive to cut through the bullshit. (I have to use this word, there isn't any other for what I mean – 'bombast' won't do it.) The wonderfully American thing about this poem is that it took this bullshit artist of the open road and made him write it so that it could become itself. I love that.

'Out of the Cradle Endlessly Rocking' is a hermetic lyric; it is of the realm of Hermes, the whisperer in the darkness, the guide of souls and the god of thieves and roadways and journeys. On the day Hermes was born he invented the lyre and stole the cattle of Apollo. To make the sound-box of the lyre he scooped a living tortoise out of its shell, he killed something to make an emptiness for his music to come out of. Then after making music he was hungry for meat so he stole Apollo's cattle.

Hermes is not officially the god of artists and the arts but he is for me: in some way there is always the killing of something to make that necessary emptiness from which the art comes and in some way the artist is always stealing what he hungers for, stealing cattle that can never be owned, cattle of beauty, cattle of truth and pain, cattle of minutes and hours – as often as not simply stealing that part of himself that is somebody else's cattle, stealing it for a secret life of finding and losing and mystery.

However it came to be there, that emptiness in Whitman wherein he heard the sea and the word from the sea is an American emptiness – you can see it in the heartbreaking summer dusk over the pines and the illuminated globes on the gas pumps in an Edward Hopper painting; you can see it in the faded lettering that says PURINA CHOWS on the side of a deserted Pennsylvania barn. Hopper and Whitman both bring their music out of that emptiness and both of them stole the cattle of themselves out of the herd of not-belonging-to self.

Hermes is the god of journeys, and that long road that passes Edward Hopper's Maine gas station is the one that America has travelled from its beginning: the spirit of America is a journeying one; everyone in America has always been on the way from one place to another, one condition to another. Our only original music comes from the descendants of slaves on their way from otherness into America's idea of itself. American blues and jazz have always in them the long road and the shining rails dwindling to a point ahead and behind; our characteristic music is always going somewhere, moving, travelling, on that train and gone with long-gone John from Bowling Green, gone with Easy Rider where the Southern meets the Yellow Dog, gone where that Midnight Special shines its light on you and me and the journeying and imprisoned soul of the Land of the Free.

How imprisoned? Like all individuals and like all nations America is a prisoner of its history, of what was done and what was not done. How many dead bodies and dead hopes has the American Dream left behind it in the domestic and foreign venues where it has played? And like all individuals and nations America is a prisoner of its own idea of itself. False legends and tall stories proliferate faster than the truth. Too often we have come blinking out of the cinema of our hopeful vanity and ridden off into the pollution tall in the saddle with John Wayne. What we truly are is a mystery to us; this mystery is continually in the process of finding a voice and for this it used Walt Whitman in his time; it used him to speak the darkness below all history and all legend, the darkness that is not only death but the womb of that mystery out of which comes new becoming.

In his chapter on Hermes in his book, *The Homeric Gods*, Walter F. Otto has this to say about the mother-darkness that is the realm of Hermes:

> A man who is awake in the open field at night or who wanders over silent paths experiences the world differently than by day. Nighness vanishes, and with it distance; everything is equally far and near, close by us and yet mysteriously remote. Space loses its measures. There are whispers and sounds, and we do not know where or what they are. Our feelings too are peculiarly ambiguous. There is a strangeness about what is intimate and dear, and a seductive charm about the frightening. There is no longer a distinction between the lifeless and the living, everything is animate and soulless, vigilant and asleep at once . . . Danger lurks everywhere . . . Who can protect him, guide him aright, give him good counsel? The spirit of Night itself, the genius of its kindliness, its enchantment, its resourcefulness, and its profound wisdom. She is indeed the mother of all mystery.

And a word from the other great Hermes-friend, Karl Kerenyi:

> For the great mystery, which remains a mystery even after all our discussing and explaining, is this: the appearance of a speaking figure, the very embodiment as it were in a human-divine form of clear, articulated, play-related and therefore enchanting, language – its appearance in that deep primordial darkness where one expects only animal muteness, wordless silence, or cries of pleasure and pain. Hermes the 'Whisperer' *(psithyristes)* inspirits the warmest animal darkness.

This also from Kerenyi:

> What he [Hermes] brings with him from the springs of creation is precisely the 'innocence of becoming'.

For me innocence of becoming is associated with the idea of the unfailed and unfailing child. This follows on my earlier thought of the grey city of failed children. Now I have to say a little more about the unfailed child. In order to do this I must go back in my thinking and my reading to the sources of this idea.

The physicist Erwin Schrodinger said:

> Mind is by its very nature a *singulare tantum*. I should say: the overall number of minds is just one. I venture to call it indestructible since it has a peculiar timetable, namely mind is always now. There is really no before and after for mind. There is only a now that includes memories and expectations.

There's no way of proving this; one can only test it against one's own experience. Does consciousness feel like that, as if there's only one mind? To me it does. I feel inhabited by a consciousness that looks out through the eyeholes in my face and this consciousness doesn't seem to have originated with me. I feel like a receiver made for a transmission that was going on long before I arrived.

It feels to me as if the total experience of the universe and every image ever imagined or seen, every word ever written or spoken, every thought ever thought is in this one mind, ceaselessly active. And I believe that whatever is in the one mind is in each of us. That being so, the total experience, not only of humanity but of the universe, is in each one of us in this one mind that is always now.

We are the children of the mystery that inhabits us and I believe that it wants us to meet it with innocence of becoming;

not to meet it is to be a failed child. Perhaps there haven't yet been any unfailed children but I think that all of us have unfailed moments. Whitman was unfailing that night on the beach; by tuning himself to the bird he entered innocence of becoming and met the mystery. And something of the American soul followed him and still follows him into the wondrous dark of it.

As if to demonstrate that they were two aspects of the same thing, Walt Whitman and Herman Melville were both born in the same year, 1819, and died in the same year, 1891. Whitman heard the song of the bird and the word from the sea on Long Island for which he used the Indian name Paumanok. Melville hunted his whale with a ship called the *Pequod*, the name of an extinct Indian tribe. It was as if each man wanted the ghosts of the original inhabitants at his back when the one invoked the savage mother and the other the white whale.

> 'Hark ye yet again, – the little lower layer,' says Ahab. 'All visible objects, man, are but as pasteboard masks. But in each event – in the living act, the undoubted deed – there, some unknown but still reasoning thing puts forth the mouldings of its features from behind the unreasoning mask. If man will strike, strike through the mask! How can the prisoner reach outside except by thrusting through the wall? To me the white whale is that wall, shoved near to me. Sometimes I think there's naught beyond. But 'tis enough. He tasks me; he heaps me; I see in him outrageous strength, with an inscrutable malice sinewing it. That inscrutable thing is chiefly what I hate; and be the white whale agent, or be the white whale principal, I will wreak that hate upon him.'

'I have written a wicked book,' said Melville in a letter to Hawthorne, 'and feel spotless as the lamb.' So far I've avoided reading any critical analyses of *Moby Dick* and I hope to continue doing so; still, I can't help wondering how much of Melville there was in Ahab and whether the Melville/Ahab balance changed after the last harpoon was thrown and the harpoon line that connected Ahab to the whale took him to his death.

The man who does battle with the unknown but reasoning thing behind the mask is dragged under by it and his mother-ship sunk. The innocent heathen Queequeg perishes with the others but his unChristian life-buoy coffin saves Ishmael:

> *Buoyed up by that coffin, for almost one whole day and night, I floated on a soft and dirge-like main. The unharming sharks, they glided by as if with padlocks on their mouths; the savage sea-hawks sailed with sheathed beaks.*

The only survivor is neither the God-maddened Ahab nor the simple savage but the civilized mariner who seems to have attained innocence of becoming. I wonder whether Melville was by then more Ishmael than Ahab, whether through his tragic and absurd hero he had purged himself of rage and recognized that his hate was a kind of love and that the duality of which one element was the enemy was in fact a unity where there was no enemy.

Moby Dick was published in 1851; 'Out of the Cradle Endlessly Rocking' wasn't until 1859; perhaps the American child had to shake its fist at the father before it could be soothed by the mother. Certainly it's a continually growing child and it seems not bound for failure, this child loving enough to beg the word of darkness from the the sea and bold enough to steer for the monstrous malevolent jaw. A promising child, I think, personified in 1884 by one Huckleberry Finn who, having written the note that will tell Miss Watson the whereabouts of the runaway slave Jim, finds himself pondering the matter:

> I felt good and all washed clean of sin for the first time I had ever felt so in my life, and I knowed I could pray now. But I didn't do it straight off, but laid the paper down and set there thinking – thinking how good it was all this happened so, and how near I come to being lost and going to hell. And went on thinking. And got to thinking over our trip down the river; and I see Jim before me, all the time, in the day, and in the night-time, sometimes moonlight, sometimes storms, and we a floating along, talking, and singing, and laughing. But somehow I couldn't seem to strike no places to harden me against him; but only the other kind. I'd see him standing my watch on top of his'n, stead of calling me, so I could go on sleeping; and see him how glad he was when I come back out of the fog; and when I come to him again in the swamp, up there where the feud was; and such-like times; and would always call me honey, and pet me, and do everything he could think of for me, and how good he always was; and at last I struck the time I saved him by telling the men we had small-pox aboard, and he was so grateful, and said I was the best friend old Jim ever had in the world, and the only one he's got now; and then I happened to look around, and see that paper.
>
> It was a close place. I took it up, and held it in my hand. I was a trembling, because I'd got to decide, forever, betwixt two things, and I knowed it. I studied a minute, sort of holding my breath, and then says to myself: 'All right, then, I'll go to hell' – and tore it up.

Huck Finn, standing alone against the authority of the failed-child establishment and refusing to sell his dark brother down the river, is about as unfailed a child as you can find: a child eminently practical and resourceful, cunning enough to survive the grey city of the world, a child in touch with the mystery of being and always in a state of innocently becoming. An American Dream with him in it has a good chance of not being a nightmare.

I said at the outset that I was going to try to find my way to the unseen part of my life that grows into and out of the American Dream. I've done what I could with that. The seen part of my life is my writing and I was late getting started. It wasn't until 1963 that I, that was a child, my tongue's use sleeping, took typewriter in hand and began to put a novel together. Since then I've tried to keep moving on that wavering edgeline where the sea of the mystery meets the strand of the more or less known, leaving my American footprints in the sand where others have walked before me, listening to the word from the waves, sometimes seeing a ghostly spout far off, and hearing always the long and lonesome whistle of the Midnight Special.

© Russell Hoban 1992

HAROLD BRODKEY
The River

PHOTOGRAPH BY HOWARD SOOLEY

Wily is fourteen, a son by adoption, a young boy 'caught in an attendant mass of realities'. It is 1944, the week of S. L.'s funeral, the only father he knew. In this extract from *The Runaway Soul*, Wily sneaks out of the apartment and bikes down to the Missouri River.

A quick glimpse through a band of dark-trunked trees of the river. Then a clear view of it across a flat, muddy field lower than the road, a field of weedy riverside corn planted in wandering, careless rows. A mighty but dowdy river back then, undammed, with visible shoals, sandbars, mud islands.

Off to the right, below the highway but higher than the field of corn, is a falling-down house, a fancy house on a knoll with a two-story side porch set between two columns, and not far from the house, under some small trees, a collapsing pergola.

Also visible (your eyes move around) is a brown unpainted barn, and then an unpainted wooden tavern with a number of neon signs already turned on, one saying FISH and another saying BEER and one announcing a local brand called OILYCOCK LAGER. In front of the tavern is a stretch of dried mud – the parking lot. Behind it is a short jetty in an inlet. Overall the place didn't have an honest look now. When we had owned this place, there had been a different barn, one painted white, with a green roof: it had been down near the river – I'd heard it had been washed away in a flood – and we'd had no tavern, no signs, no parking lot, just trees and grass and farm fields. We'd often parked on grass.

I hid my bike in a copse near the road, in the muck under a fallen locust; I covered it with fallen branches. I took off my jeans so I was in the cut-off jeans I'd put on underneath at home.

I left the long jeans with the bike under the branches and I made my way through the woods walking in a stream in my sneakers – the stream which wound down (through often tall banks) to the inlet. Ignoring the flies and mosquitoes – the bugs – I walked along, stung-legged, wet-legged, odd-mooded, now with the sky visible, now with it hidden. At the mouth of the stream, where it emptied into the inlet, under willows, lay a very large, ungainly river dinghy. It was greenish and heavy, made of thick and heavy pieces of wood, scarred and scratched, peeling, and warped, moored to a ring in the trunk of a willow. Dilapidated and poor. I step into the sloshing water in the boat. In that water are warped, unpainted oars; I lift one and figure, sadly, they are too big for me to row with but I can use one as a pole in the muddy bottom shallows. We'd owned this boat once. I untied it. The boat moves slowly in smelly water. I was uneasy, then afraid. Then the fear was tremendous in me and only laziness and self-doubt kept me from giving up . . . I could see how some men wore out young. As S.L. had.

The clay of the banks, the yellow marl, had dirty red and loose-edged brown stripes and ovals in it. Past decrepit and mournful willows, I poled, tense with adventure. At the spreading mouth of the inlet, only a little current is present, guarded by a sandbank, shoals, and an island of reeds a hundred and fifty yards off shore. The ripples of the currents of a sensible river move here – it is not as it is in my head later in New York, years later, ostensibly present in the dry mind, a slop of fluids and electric traces. A real river is not uncertainly mounted in space but is actually there.

I poled out into the shoaled water where real current was possible, but it was possible the water would be calm. It looked calm. At the edge of the reeds, which rose maybe sixteen feet into the air, I tied the dinghy to a log, half buried in the mud. And I climbed out of the boat into the muddy water; I feel my lower legs moistly muddied in the water . . . my bare feet are in the gooey mud of the bottom . . . river molluscs cut my feet and river shrimp tickle my ankles. My feet and lower legs are as if murmuring with sensation. My gym shoes, their laces tied, are around my neck. The quick pulsations of fear and the alternating and, maybe, ruling bravery, or recklessness, and the thing of how it felt to be really alone for a change, the expansion of the mind then – as if your own mind became a mother or a brother there with you for the day, going along with you for the day's stuff – and to be alone in this wobbly state of bravery with no audience, I had come here for this but hadn't remembered from before what it was really like . . . The reeds towered over my head, and the mud flats and the muck of shallow river water smelled. To be frank, it was really creepy. As I said, the Missouri was undammed then, was a loosened and natural river, a naturally occuring, shoally, sloppy, weird thing, wet and wide, flat-surfaced, twisty with currents, big, unsafe.

Among the reeds, the water was combed and rendered into glass, stilled. I waded into the reeds, which walled in the eye. They themselves had tickling odors as the water did, the stifling air, and the muck did, too. So did I, I smelled, too, by now, the motionful wader in the stilled water, smelled with nerves, and heat, with grief, and of the river. One's mind moves in the endowment of silence – and in that quietness feels how hot it was in that odd grove and how it really stank there. The thin shimmer of dankness that rose gassily among the reeds in the shadow-strips and light and the odor – and bars and blobs of light and the thin shadows and the smell; it was sticky . . . the bugs bit. In a way, it was like being indoors, in the reed-columned roofless room – no rooms and reed-walled, wet corridors. I walked testingly observant for sinkholes and snapping turtles. In the striped brightness, the stippling on my arms of brightly lit tiny blond hairs and the precise shadows they cast were ordinary nature which meant me: a *hunh* of loud breathing: a raw madness . . . different from home: not a domestic madness: my breath moves differently; I feel my ribs inside my skin; my degree of strength – physical strength – is a constant issue here of life and death, or life and injury, and not of politeness and murder, as at home, or whatever it is there. The rawness of being a self is kind of raucous here. A nervous, crowlike cawing, an intruder thing is what my identity feels like. I don't know. I turned over *in my head* (and partly in my chest and throat) the idea of swimming out into the river – *a fifty-fifty chance* of drowning – 'fifty-fifty' was rhetorical: I didn't know what the odds were. After a few minutes, I felt myself running out of courage – I had minced my dad's not being entirely courageous about his own dying. I had forgotten that that was so about courage, that it ran out, that it was subject to being used up: it burned in the friction of the moments and went out. I maybe partly understood a little about the ways my father had gotten tired of life, of courage. What he had meant when he said he was tired, what he'd meant when he'd said my mother – or I or my sister, Nonie (his real daughter, not adopted) – had ground him down, worn him out, had used up his courage. He said those things; those were his phrases. The reeds rustled in a passing wind. He sometimes used words like *guts, courage, class, a fighting heart, a Fighter's Heart* (like Man o' War's or Jack Dempsey's). He said that pushing yourself to your limit, and so on, destroyed your heart; don't do it, he said. I didn't want to commit suicide, but I was accustomed to turning things over to *chance*, to my darker self – selves – and seeing what the vote was, seeing what happened. I did want to die . . . but maybe not entirely.

I made myself be brave again. I knew from the odor kind of freshening itself and becoming a kind of sweet stink and then not so much a stink at all but merely clinging and wet and riverine, and from a difference in the heat, a lessening of it, and a sound like a rumble growing louder, that I was approaching, in the bed of reeds, a limit of the privacy and that I was coming to the unobstructed river. I wasn't sure what I was coming to. I should have said I had some warning before I came out of the rustling discontinuum of reeds at the rim of a great, immediate circle of wide, hurrying, gray-colored water. And sky. A scene of peculiar radiance, that immense showy grayness: a brute enormity, an enormous scene of water, an everywhere of hurrying water and of reflections . . . giant reflections: in places, a gigantic expanse of river that rippled and that was inset with vast reflections of clouds moving on the hurrying water. The reflections shifted curlingly.

Impressed and dubious toward the natural glory and its plainness and its dangerousness, I trailed a hand in the light-struck, unstable, hurrying surface as if to restore a sensory narrowness of perception, but I felt the water moving and wrapping itself around me, my fingers, and the palms and backs of my hands and wrists; and the merciless transience, insatiable-throated and sulphurous-muddy, on my hands or in them, my wrists were half clasped by it; the stench-ridden, flowing and unobliging, gliding pliability and wet suffocation of the water. The reality held me and then dragged me out into the middle of the river and then, oh, two hundred feet into the air. Aerially, I felt the, uh, goddamned, remorseless replacement of everything, the air, the water, every moment, by itself, itself a moment later; so that everything is in a different moment but it's not the same everything, it's only the same everything in an unfocused way, somehow, because it's a moment later. Have you noticed it's a different moment all the time? The marvelously undulant atoms and electrons and this mysterious other motion — or the same one — but it's like blinks and flights of attention . . . in gallopingly fluid cantos, stanzas: the motions of things. You FEEL the air on your lips rhyme itself from a few seconds ago. The earlier state has skedaddled away. And this moment, this n-o-w, is not clearly formed, it's not still; hardly alit; it hasn't alit; it's fluttering; but it's still n-o-w, but it's a different now, loosely or wildly different.

A river-borne tree trunk, dipping and twirling, sodden, with some roots and leafy branches on it still, went by thirty feet away from me. It would have broken my back if it had hit me. So I thought of the drowning of everything in being newly everything all the time and still, continuingly, drowning in being attached somehow — a mysterious spine of twirling, bodiless vertebrae . . . I saw stuff arrive at the surface of the river near the hurrying water around my legs, real stuff, but I felt the moment doing stuff, and I felt the stuff of moments doing stuff in me as well, becoming everything or taking its place eerily, coming and going; and I became recalcitrant; I became slowed pools of watchfulness in motion and watching everything be in motion, eddying without surface or bottom or banks. And the reflections, the *thoughts* were like clocks, and had tides and were slowed and recalcitrant pools as well . . . And what was watching ticked, too, and moved and swept along and was swept or stood still and flowered and died and kept going in some way or other.

But it was too hard — and too immodest — to do this. Instead, I *felt* time to be held in my silently blowing-bellows-like taut lungs — and in my hair and in the belly wall and in my toes in the mud underwater, but I was separate, too, so that I was a *committee* of times and hours and of timelessness anchored and unanchored chronographically in ways taught in school, a ribbed and breathing steeple made of whirring clocks, whirring clocks for eyes and stiller ones for the inner eyes and clocks, also, of my breathing and, differently, of my memory of breathing if I looked at myself breathing a moment ago . . . And then I gave up the timelessness; and life seemed an AMBITION — of, something like the nature of time itself with its direction fixed — to be known in-my-blood now as a spirit of individual chaos humming or whistling along ambitiously in a universal tick-tock and bustle. So that I was, oh, sort of, time in a bag and forked at the crotch — the bag was time, too, and was blowing along and the mind was rolling along, one member of a congress of sightednesses, all of them awhistle with time.

I felt, maybe stupidly, the humming and whistling inside my lips and of my lips — breaths, atoms — atoms? — and the molecules of my breath, oxygen-drained and monoxide-ridden or whatever — but all of us, me, and all of me, and the river, flying along mysteriously, ticking and breathing, into being and being in this flowering surf and eerie tide.

The wish to continue the world, to have it continue as an *I-am-alive* reality in itself, in no degree or jot or iota separate from what couldn't be named as me (there was no place apart from it for me to name it from), was crudely different now — everything in its reality, bustling, hurtling, ticking, hymning and humming along . . . in fraught *ambition* — like my own breathing throat and its ambition to continue to breathe . . . Or a molecule or atom or electron existing . . . But more pervasive and single and not exactly different as muscle and blood and tendons were from each other — and trachea and neck bones and hair on the nape from hair on my crotch. I didn't think I was a prophet or that I had been given a message, or, rather, I did wonder about that, but I doubted that it would matter to a lot of people, what I'd thought or what had happened here — I doubted that I was a big-time prophet . . . I couldn't think this was a historical moment.

I did think, pretentiously, *Well, try to be important, Wiley.* I thought that what was weirdest about time being everywhere was that if it was everywhere, if it was universal, then God was biographical and had a history, whether I could understand it or not.

I felt a radiance spread in me equal, in minor terms, of a maybe only mildly successful orgasm during masturbation, but not from trying to think about that last thing, but from the kind of meaning earlier, more a sense of meaning than a meaning formulated. Then, this sense of meaning in the bustling and hurried universe, this sense of a sense available to ME, I located (a certain actual image of it) in my mildly convulsed throat with its various labors of supporting the skull and of angling and twisting to aim the eyes and ears while it worked away at carrying blood and air in this heat. A throat. A throat. Then that faded into a mob of *clocks* that stare at each other and overlap and tug and flower in a great brouhaha. It is very like music. I have an inward shout of GOD WHAT AM I TO DO ABOUT THIS? I wasn't told what to do about it. I thought, *Well, shove it up your ass, Wiley* . . . I waited, not with a lot of hope; but I wasn't told anything. Shyly prophetic — since no project was given me — I told myself to *back off, quiet down, button up*: it would mean too much trouble, it would cause too much trouble to argue or believe what I myself thought — to lay claim to meaning. But it seemed to me that I saw the shadows on the water, and in the ones in the depths and those cast by the ripples, a dot or an egg, sort of a mirroring thing, that I did believe and would hold onto as belief. People had said to me, *Don't ever believe yourself, Wiley.*

In the nowhere inside my head — that unperpetual everywhere — the nowhere-but-there in my head kept claiming an apartness from time — but it now had a belief that what was truly *out there* was a papery and rustling and crumpling NOW with an unresolved arriving as well as a steadily observable moving off of it, both the old moment and the new moment, not in sequence, but eccentrically or syncopatedly overlapped, the complexly shaped n-o-w; and that this was so in me as well, and was so of my thoughts and ideas. I did believe this – but not all parts of me believed it – my mind itself, my very *mind*, kept insisting on being apart from the motion.

Well, I still had my hand in the water, and then I bent my head back and opened my eyes to the air – sort of waiting for a sign, you know? – but the touch of the water on my hand touched me flickeringly; and then I was high, high up again; and it seemed to me that moments don't move physically quite; it's spiritual; anyway, they simply fail to pause in place even while they seem to present themselves in an almost knowable *courtesy*, as if they did pause.

But they are unroofed, unfloored, even if stiffly (or stilly) present. *Please-forgive-me*, the air whispered . . . And the part of the mind cut off from the regular mind, the part of the mind that thought this said *Please forgive me* to the other part, which didn't think it and never accepted it, the divinely unstable – and ferocious and devouring – and illusory stillness-of-other-motion of the motion of the moments.

Dreamlike! Dreamlike! The nearer air and the farther air and a further air of a notion, and somehow the sky flittering and receding (when you look at it), the separate pieces of the softly oozing everywhere in its unresting flowering. This dwarfed me: mad, madding, maddening NATURE – and time in it . . . Big deal . . . I got mixed up: I was studying Virgil and Horace in school, and Abraham (Abe) Lincoln in history, and physics and geometry and English; and in English class, Thomas Hardy and George Eliot and Notions of Fate in the English Countryside. I was actually studying what teachers said those writers said they saw . . . I figured I wasn't having a vision. I was trying to join some kind of band of people who didn't have dead fathers and who had opinions about the countryside.

I felt the humming and buzzing in my ears and legs as well as in my lips and lungs, and I felt it in my certitudes and grief, in my errors . . . the humming of time *everywhere*.

In and above and around and under the shaking river – and my mind blinkingly dreaming – real time and me, I'm made of time. I take on an immediacy; I take my hand out of the water; I hear my mother's and my sister's and my father's voices: *You're a fool. You sound like a fool. You were always a fool . . . I have no time for your crazy ideas . . .* They and I say in separate tones, *Leave me alone.*

I say it out loud to the sky . . . I say out loud, *Leave me alone. I don't believe it . . . I don't believe it is this simple . . .*

I don't know if I do believe it or not . . . *I don't want to think about it anymore:* Incomprehensibly linked (not end-to-end but overlapping) and unstoppable moments – never a nothingness, never stillness – a universe of such restlessness that it explains everything – but if it explains EVERYTHING, what good is it?

Come off it. What's the Big Idea? Don't make me laugh.

The shuddering plenum, is it true? *Don't listen to yourself. Stay sane.*

You can't have a nothingness in which everything buzzingly moves, can you? I think it is possible that GOD never retreats from the birth of consciousness onward, from being surrounded by, immersed in, the restless ambition of everything, all the trash tyrants hooting and hollering and going boo and whistling and singing along.

This moment was like being blown up but not killed, partly explained instead and filled with a radiance of sorts. But it seems fatal.

Leaning hayricks of revolving and variedly colored rays of sunlight – oblique, slanted – come through lit-up holes in the cloud cover and touch the gray, current-tickled surface of the water. Weird bird shadows move skimmingly on the lit and shadowed melted lid of the currents. The shadows skippingly skid, without sound, across the visible patterns of movements of the water. Birds, a water hawk – a river eagle, maybe – and three fish crows – bird eyes, bird feathers, whatever – chirring and sudden – their reflections are legible, are recognizably of a species. Motored with appetite and directed by habit and in the lovely and grotesque oppressions of both, they appear and vanish and then reappear as they move in the sky. They are never more than partly visible. But their reflections are legible.

HELP ME.

The eerie truth and lopsided song is that the gross outer shells of the world twist and gleam and darken, and I believe in nothing, not in them, not in me. Only in death and in youth for the time being. Unconcluded truth shifts in me in the varying light. Breath moves a bit kissingly in the rolling passages of the minutes . . . It is okay to be wrong. It's part of who I am the way the shape or the movement of wings is part of a family of birds. The eyelid thing of blinking and thinking in the middle of a stinking river. Proof is different from this.

Light and clouds and the shadows on the water, the birds overhead, their cries and skimming reflections, the boy, the reeds, the shore, the truth, the error – all of it exists here in the many-winged flutter and mutter in the moment. It flies to nowhere. It moves motionlessly into unexistencehood in actual moments where I am still, like a phonograph needle, noticing the deviations that become the course of argument of the thoughtlight in my mind. It becomes memory – usefulness – a flag, a cloudy thought. I stand in the struggling flowing rot of the river. I think (or feel) this stuff months before willing to argue it with Remsen (a friend at school who sometimes sucks me off) and years, decades before I will be willing to write about it. Illusions of God, delusions – hallucination – confusion on confusion. I will say to Remsen: *I'm not brave enough to be crazy.*

We don't know enough about the world to speak of it conclusively so far.

I will say to Remsen, *We don't know enough to be dogmatic, you asshole . . .*

But that's in the future . . .

© Harold Brodkey 1991

DAVID RIEFF

LOS ANGELES

CAPITAL OF THE THIRD WORLD

IN L.A., ALL THE RACES OF THE
WORLD ARE FIELDING THEIR TEAMS.

PHOTOGRAPHS BY ANTHONY HERNANDEZ

The labor-saving devices that transformed America – all those vacuum cleaners, electric ranges, dishwashers, and the like – look smaller now. To approach them with the same wonder that young couples did in the forties and fifties is no more possible than returning as an adult to the house one lived in as a child and not being disappointed by its diminution. And yet these were the devices that had permitted an America victorious in the World War to create a society that, materially at least, seemed on the cutting edge of the modern. It was a world of homes and roads, home appliances and automobiles. And if Los Angeles had invented neither the garden suburb nor the freeway, the fifties idea of domestic 'togetherness' nor the outlying residential shopping mall, it was Los Angeles that took this world of things, and the world of feeling that accompanied it, to its logical conclusion: perfecting it, in the eyes of its boosters; creating a barren, homogenized conformity, in the opinion of its critics.

Everyone understands what the automobile did to change the United States, but most underestimate the effect of the washing machine. It was home appliances that made the garden ideal of the suburb different in the fifties. Suburbs, after all, were an old American trope, and the ideas about the caring, not to say self-absorbed, family that most people associate with the fifties were in fact much older. The fear of the dangerous city, often peopled by aliens and nonwhites, as well as the ideal of suburban domesticity, was well in place by 1900. The idea of life as a species of amusement was also nothing new. A 1923 brochure offering tract homes in the L.A. suburb of Palos Verdes advertised that this was a town where 'your home is your playground'.

What was different was that there was a surfeit of things, and, as their effects were felt, a surfeit of time. Chores that had previously required a week of work were diminished, in the shiny postwar world, to the effort of a single day. It was women, many of whom were entering the labor force for the first time and whose paychecks had permitted so many couples to acquire their dream houses, who had to find this time. That meant evenings and weekends, mostly, since their husbands, when they contributed at all, only mowed the lawn – increasingly on motorized mowers – or set the sprinklers. Father knows best, indeed.

But Dad and Mom alike were increasingly coming to view life less as a playground than as a supermarket, which, in fact, at a time when they were few and far between in the rest of the country, had been commonplace in Southern California since the early thirties. It was the volume of demand that made the fifties extraordinary and explains the hold they still have on the imaginations of those who grew up in them. The children in

Geoffrey O'Brien's brilliant memoir of the counterculture, *Dream Time*, are described as living in 'a civilization that brought them things. They could count on a new crop of toys each Christmas, always a little more technologically advanced than last year's models: tin robots that spoke and walked, plastic rockets with a range of up to thirty feet. New television programs were provided each September to set the tone for that autumn's play, whether the props were Davy Crockett hats or Zorro capes or a rifle like Chuck Connors used.'

People wanted more, more things and more for themselves. The enchantment with children, which had seemed such a permanent feature during the 1950s, when all the polls showed women rating their children as the greatest satisfaction of their lives, faded. In fact, the baby boom had been an anomaly, and, plotted over the course of the entire twentieth century, the demographic arrow of white American fertility moves steadily down. The cheap buildings put up by developers and the cheap loans offered by the Bank of America and its imitators may have lured people to the suburbs and instilled in them a limitless taste for buying, but they felt lonely in these suburbs, the men complaining of feeling hemmed in, the women, now working in increasing numbers, of being stifled. This is the world that Betty Friedan described so well in *The Feminine Mystique*, the world that Gloria Steinem believed offered only a stark choice between motherhood and selfhood, 'I either gave birth to someone else,' she recalled of her decision not to have children, 'or I gave birth to myself.'

The solipsism of the middle class, as the social historian Barbara Ehrenreich has called it, may have permitted people not to think about the consequences of the system they had created for the longest time. By the same token, the mistaken impression in the United States – that most solipsistic of nations – that it exists not just outside history but outside geography as well (witness the country's historic indifference to Mexico, along with Canada the only country in the world with whose destiny that of the U.S. is *permanently* linked) has led it to mistake its postwar prosperity for a permanent condition, for a right. All this is understandable, of course, even America's ahistoricity the paradoxical product of its specific history. What is extraordinary is that the democratic capitalism of California, which at its core is nihilistic in the dictionary sense of believing all traditional values and systems baseless, could imagine itself and persuade others that it stood for something that could be passed on to posterity.

If people were to devote themselves to making money and amassing possessions, not to speak of – here, the ethos of the counterculture and that of cowboy capitalism did indeed coincide – giving birth to themselves, to use Steinem's extraordinary phrase, they were unlikely to have time to clean up after themselves as well. A life spent on the job, in the gym, between the sheets, or in the mall can only be lived with a staff. Men have always known this: that was one of the reasons so many resisted, in the sixties and seventies (before brute economic necessity – the inability of a middle-class couple to live on a single paycheck), the idea of their wives going out to work. Now, what many younger professional women were referring to as a postfeminist generation were discovering that the problem was, if anything, more acute if you were single.

Maids were the obvious solution, the 'Leave It to Beaver' sitcom world of a preceding generation having been replaced by a 'thirtysomething' world (but a realistic one, this time) of 'leave it to the maid'. Life was quite literally described by many people I met as being impossible without the enabling presence of these maids, cooks, and gardeners. It was one thing to work long hours at something you cared about, or to devote yourself to a sport or a hobby. But there was no way as long as they could afford it that a generation that had grown up thinking of life as, essentially, fun was going to be reconciled to mopping their own floors or cleaning their own toilets. Somebody had to, though, usually somebody whose last name ended with a *z*, an *a*, or an *o*.

Once, when Allegra – with whom I was living in L.A. – wanted a week alone to bull her way through, uninterrupted, the rewrite of her script, I went to stay with friends in a beautiful house in Brentwood Park. They had an enormous dog, a Hungarian puli with hair like a catastrophe in a dust mop factory, and a sweet and clownish disposition, that I took to walking at improbable hours, as much to make my way around the unfamiliar neighborhood on foot as for any more altruistic motive. This need for a pretext was real. With fear of crime rampant – it was said that criminals from South Central L.A. referred to the Westside and the Valley as the 'lands', for lands of opportunity – neighborhoods like Brentwood were a sea of barred windows and octagonal signs planted in the shrubbery or rose borders that read, WESTEC SECURITY: ARMED RESPONSE.

When I would go out in the early morning, the streets would be empty, but by the time the dog and I would begin pantingly to make our way home, we would pass those telltale beat-up old station wagons and pickup trucks. Slowing to a halt, these vehicles would disgorge their cargoes of small, brown-skinned men. In silence, they would set to work, mowing the lawns, trimming the opulent hedges, seeing to the sprinkler systems, and sweeping up the natural debris – palm fronds, eucalyptus leaves, and the like – that Los Angeles discharges on even the most windless of its evenings. But if, by 8:00 a.m., the streets of Brentwood were filled with these gardeners and, as Katharine Hepburn might have said in *The Philadelphia Story*, groundskeepers, by noon they had vanished. Sometime in the interim, it appeared, the men had either walked to the bus stop on San Vicente Boulevard to begin the hours-long trek back to East Los Angeles by RTD, or else they had been collected by the same beat-up old jalopies that had delivered them to the Westside in the first place.

People who have never lived in Los Angeles tend to suppose that everything there is so green and luxuriant because the place is some kind of natural arboretum. The opposite is true, and the maintenance of West L.A.'s sparkling appearance is an extremely difficult, labor-intensive activity. The Californian natural paradise lies in the northern part of the state, not in the Los Angeles basin, a desert ringed by the Pacific, the mountains, and that much-fetishized epiphenomenon of plate tectonics known as the San Andreas Fault. A short flight over the area on a clear day is proof enough, but there is another journey, this time by car, that makes the point even more vividly. For you only have to drive two hours south to Tijuana, across the Mexican border in the province of Baja California, to get a proper sense of what Beverly Hills and Brentwood would be were they not constantly tended by armies of hired Latino help. The streets of what is, in fact, one of the most prosperous cities in Mexico are dusty and ill-kempt, having the benefit neither of gardeners (they've all gone north to work) or the stolen water of the Owens Valley to make them green, peaceful, and alluring.

Bewitched by the dryness of the climate, visitors sometimes imagine that the Los Angeles basin is such an exception to the laws of botany that all those luxurious plants they see growing in their friends' gardens would do so if left wild. As for Angelenos themselves, they too often speak as if they have forgotten the real reasons their backyards look the way they do. To be sure, people routinely fret about the water shortage, but to talk about the future in even the most apocalyptic terms is by no means the same thing as apprehending the present. The fear of fire, which every sane L.A. homeowner has in his bones, presses on even daily conversation. Except among passionate environmentalists, anxieties about the aqueducts and the drought do not. In Los Angeles, a garden is a garden, a water problem is a water problem, and connections between the two remain tenuous at best.

Left, CHRIST LOVES YOU, right, BLANKET HOUSE; immigrant encampments beneath the Harbor Freeway, downtown Los Angeles, 1991

There is also the small matter of Hollywood. A city this long in the business of manufacturing illusions can hardly be expected to encourage its residents to peek behind the stage set. In any case, there is the stubborn hope that if a solution cannot be found, at least the moment when one has to come to grips with the problem can be deferred. In the meantime, it was best to pay the brown people whose elbow grease maintained the illusion, and enjoy the show. Still, the obliviousness could be breathtaking. 'You don't have to do any work to get things to grow here,' a scriptwriter friend of Allegra's told us, as we sat by his pool in the late afternoon sunlight.

Allegra, who as a Northern Californian by birth knew better, winked at me. She had seen me, earlier during lunch, as I watched the gardener gather his things and let himself out through the garden gate at the far end of the pool.

'Yeah, right,' she said, spearing an endive leaf, 'and I'll bet your teeth brush themselves as well.' There was the usual embarrassed silence that falls over West L.A. social gatherings when people say something harsh that cannot be explained away by its connection to work. Indeed, exceptions to this attitude were rare. When Tim Rutten, an editorial page writer at the *Los Angeles Times* (who would eventually become my closest friend in Los Angeles) told me that his mother refused to hire maids, and insisted that as long as her husband and sons sat at her table, they could do the household chores for themselves, I was not surprised when he added quickly that his mother was literally the only person he was aware of who still hewed to such an old-fashioned conception of domestic responsibilities. More common was the presumption that there would always be some unknown person to take care of the dirty bits of life. Once, as I chatted with a friend of Allegra's about her new baby, and asked her how her life was different, she replied, 'Oh, it changes your life, all right.' Then, pausing for a moment and shaking her head ruefully she added, 'I mean, it changes someone's life; I mean it changes some Guatemalan's life.' She meant the remark as a joke, of course, but, after she had delivered it, she shifted uncomfortably, as if its truth had only then become clear to her, and swept off into the kitchen to pour herself another cup of coffee. When she returned, we talked about German reunification.

It was hard to see, however, any way that in the longer term the realities of the situation could be covered up by such jokes or the more usual bland denials. Whites on the Westside of Los Angeles had grown accustomed to delegating even some of the most important aspects of their lives to hired immigrant enablers. Every year, the degree to which the real facts of daily life were at odds with the way middle-class people understood their experience increased. To leave one's office in Century City or Beverly Hills and know that the trashcans were emptied and the floors mopped down was one thing; you didn't have to see the janitors who did that work, and, indeed, the janitors' strike in Century City in 1990 probably succeeded because the strikers, by roaming through the complex rather than picketing outside and by entering nearby yuppie watering holes at happy hour, made themselves visible. But it was quite another thing to live alongside the people who were picking up after you and caring for your children.

Everything had changed in a generation. Even an activity as recreational as gardening has been transformed, in L.A., into one that requires the services of a gardener. But that was no problem. Los Angeles is now a place where a middle-class person can live in a First World way for Third World prices, at least for domestic help. With illegal immigrant laborers, many of whom had worked on farms in Mexico before coming north, in abundant supply, there was no shortage of able hands willing to work for next to nothing. For the middle class of the Westside, this meant that a style of life that had been the preserve of the truly rich was now within reach. When people spoke about the work that had one into their gardens, it was almost invariably mostly someone else's work. When they spoke about the rigors of child-rearing, they rarely meant coping with the wash, or, after infancy, with the long, wearing afternoons only a fractious toddler can produce. All in all, such talk was eerily reminiscent of a horsebreeder at a yearling sale or puffing with pride in the winner's circle after a race. No one expects a horse owner, no matter how proudly he may speak of 'his' horse, to have mucked out the stable beforehand, or even to have ridden in the race. The speech of the rich, however, has always been riddled with the ghosts of absent servants. Now, in L.A., the speech of the middle class is as well.

It struck me that the United States was beginning to look like the world as it is presented in that sublime Japanese theater form Bunraku. Bunraku is a puppet theater. Dressed in sumptuous kimonos, the puppet characters are moved around the stage by a group of masked black-clad handlers while their costumes are changed by other members of the company who crouch at the back of the set, new miniature kimonos at the ready. The audience is aware that the puppets are being manipulated by these two groups of enablers (there is no attempt at concealment or darkening of the stage), but it is understood that what matters is the action of the drama. The stories are familiar, classics from the same repertoire drawn on by the Kabuki and Noh theaters. What makes Bunraku so odd and so remarkable is that it is one of the few theatrical forms in which people appear on stage, fully visible, and yet are, at most, of purely secondary interest to an audience. While we may admire the dexterity of a particular handler – they exist, they can be seen – from the spectator's standpoint, they are invisible as well (or, at least, they scarcely signify).

Something similar has taken place in Southern California. Without all the immigrants willing to do the menial work that native-born Americans (including most blacks, much as some of their leaders deny it) have forsworn, no cars would get parked at Westside restaurants, no lawns would be tended, and no infants looked after. Their employers, though, hardly acknowledge their existence, while for every Anglo child who grows attached to the maid another is confused by her presence. 'I was alone all day,' the five-year-old daughter of one of Allegra's friends told me boastfully. 'The maid was there,' her mother interjected, 'but she only speaks Spanish and the child thinks she won't talk to her on purpose.'

'That's right,' the girl piped up, 'I was alone with no one to talk to.'

To Anglo L.A., nothing could be more present and yet nothing more shadowy than the lives of these servants. They are as ignored as puppet handlers, as opaque and incomprehensible as the obscurest of Stone Age hunters deep in the Brazilian rain forest. At least the aboriginal peoples of the Amazon have their backers on the Westside, people who raise money for them, give parties for them, and otherwise champion their cause. The maids have no such cachet. But then, the lives of servants never carry much weight in the minds of those who employ them. It is a natural enough conceit, rather like believing that the lives of actors, even when they are only inanimate Bunraku puppets, invariably must outshine the lives of the maids and butlers who dress and undress them, and facilitate their progress across the stage, their footsteps muffled by the background music of beautiful old songs.

A few noticed the incongruity, even if they did not quite know where to move it from there. The first time I met Tim Rutten, we had lunch at one of the fine new restaurants that have cropped up in Los Angeles during the course of the past fifteen years. City, on La Brea and Second, is a great barn of a place, looking from some angles like a converted aircraft hangar, from other vantage points like an art gallery. A video monitor over the bar showing the work in the kitchens adds to the impression of taking in a performance piece along with lunch. Toward the end of the meal I had with Tim, when the busboy, whose face could have served as the model for a Mayan sculptor in the age of Tikal or Chichén Itzá, came to clear away our plates, I found myself staring at him for longer than was civil.

'You've got it,' Tim said, catching my eye. 'This town runs on brown wheels.' And it seemed appropriate that, as happens so often in Southern California, even the most uncomfortable act of understanding and imaginative sympathy came wrapped in the fizzy vernacular of the automobile.

If you were to follow Wilshire Boulevard from where it begins, a few blocks away from the Santa Monica Pier in a part of town local wags have christened 'Croissant Canyon', sixteen miles east to where it peters out, a nondescript street bounded by construction sites and the impassive chrome and steel towers of that far steeper canyon otherwise known as downtown L.A., you would have made your way across neighborhoods in which all the races of the world have fielded their teams. Look a little closer and it does indeed seem as if Los Angeles has been busy fulfiling Walt Whitman's prescient remark in the preface of *Leaves of Grass* that the United States would soon become the 'nation of nations . . . race of races'. That drive from the edge of the Pacific to the lobby of the Security Pacific Bank building is actually a perfect story-board version, as the locals say, this being scriptwriter country, of the ethnic present of California and, perhaps, the ethnic future of the whole country.

A full quarter of all non-native-born Americans, the overwhelming majority of whom had come from East Asia and Latin America, now lived in California. They had not been lured to Los Angeles or Silicon Valley around San Jose by high-tech jobs, as had immigrants from other parts of the United States, but rather had come, in search of a better life, or drawn by the lure of America, or fleeing war and hunger, in ever greater numbers since the 1965 revision of a previously racist immigration law had permitted the first large-scale admission of nonwhite peoples to the United States since the early part of the century. It was true, of course, that these new immigrants were often living better in L.A. than they would have back home, but not only were many of them not doing well, often they were barely surviving. But they didn't vote, and except on the six o'clock news, with its lurid assemblage of crime and arson in the precincts where the poor lived, they were as invisible to white California (except, perhaps, in its nightmares) as they were to the politicians.

If Los Angeles was indeed, as its enthusiasts proclaimed, the capital of a new 'United States of California' – and there was, in any case, something a little off about this talk of the California Republic as a potential if not an actual reality rather than just some words written at the bottom of the state flag, under the bear and the star – that new nation was at least as much part of the Third World as the First, and growing more so every day. A simple drive downtown would have confirmed this fact for white Angelenos, but that was the rub. There was no reason for anyone to go there, except to work or to take in an occasional show at the Music Center. And even those incursions were, by and large, a matter of interiors – cars, parking garages, auditoriums, and restaurants.

The maids, of course, crossed the city regularly. But when they did so they were more or less by themselves. One saw them, sitting patiently on the big orange buses of the Los Angeles Rapid Transit Department, being ferried back and forth between their homes in East L.A. and those of their employers. Frequently the only other riders were a few old Anglos too infirm now to drive their cars, some black or Latino school kids, and the odd drunk slumped, snoring, in the rear. White Los Angeles knew nothing of these buses. Indeed, to ride one would have been an act almost as preposterous as shimmying up one of the palm trees that tower on the median strips of the boulevards. Like those bits of exogenous vegetation, the buses are a visual constant but no more – like back projection in a movie.

During the time I spent in L.A., I met no one on the Westside who had been on an RTD bus more than once or twice in their lives. One person admitted to knowing of someone who used the system, but this turned out to be a French student at USC who had failed the California driving test three times already and was gearing up, as we spoke, for a fourth attempt by spending every spare dollar she had at a local driving school.

Not that there was any reason for someone with a driver's license to use public transportation. The RTD buses are slow, their air-conditioning breaks down often, and even if they take you in the general vicinity of where you're going, that proximity is relative. More often than not, you still have to walk another mile or two to get to the actual street address. And there can be few experiences more disconcerting than walking along a wide L.A. street without the reassuring jangle of car keys in your pocket. Those streets are largely unshaded, their sidewalks appearing wider because they are so empty. The traffic lights, timed for vehicles rather than pedestrians, pose a menace to the scattered largely geriatric population of pedestrians, so much so, in fact, that the impression is inescapable that the advertisements you see on benches all over the Westside for Jewish funeral chapels are really messages aimed at anyone foolish enough to expect to long survive as a walker in Los Angeles.

To move around the city on foot is like being lost in the desert that the Los Angeles basin once was, and will doubtless become again, or like floating in space. The bare concrete surfaces and the hard, flat light only underscore the sense of being adrift and at risk, even if the particular neighborhood you find yourself in is safe and its geography apparent to you. For the new immigrants, the impression must be magnified many times over. They are easy to spot, these recent arrivals from south of the border, walking along aimlessly – or is it just that they still have a long way to go? – under street signs they are far from likely to be able to decipher. Sometimes they move in complete family units, paunchy, dignified men, haggard women, and a train of children taking up the rear. Sometimes, they walk alone, in this city the size of Neptune.

It was one thing for me to heed these brown faces on the streets or attend to the breathtaking mix of languages, a lower-middle-class immigrant Babel, on the shop fronts of the mini-malls. If I learned to copy out, though not decipher, the stolid rectangles of Korean Hankul script and the florid curlicues of Thai and Armenian, that was, after all, part of what had drawn me to Los Angeles in the first place. But it was hardly the way that anybody who is not a writer (or, conceivably, a policeman or a social worker) could be expected to want to spend what – in Los Angeles, which despite its reputation, is one of the least laid back places in the world – is laughably called their 'free time'.

I had come alone to a city for which I felt much affection but little familiarity, eager to soak up every last picturesque drop of daily life there. But what for me was, of necessity, the center of my days and nights in L.A. seemed to most of my friends at best a strange but largely irrelevant background noise to their daily lives. The writer has no fixed hours on the road. When Tim Rutten and I would drive, as we often did, back from the *Times* building downtown to what his wife laughingly described as their home in the 'slums' of Hancock Park, he was finished with his working day, whereas I might have accomplished nothing of any use to my project, only to suddenly reach for my notebook, jarred into inspiration by something glimpsed as we drove past – two Salvadoran children lunging toward a soccer ball in the front yard of a run-down housing court on Sixth and Occidental; the name of a Korean Presbyterian Church on Wilshire; or winos lined up in front of a blood bank in downtown L.A., hard under the shadow of the upscale Bunker Hill apartment complex whose construction had destroyed so much of the single room occupancy housing which, before the real estate boom, had sheltered some of them from the cruelties of the streets.

In Los Angeles, it seemed, even nature was on the march. According to one news report, the United States was being invaded by what was referred to as 'worldwide transfers of immigrant plant species' that might well eventually crowd out 'the natives'. Though the story ended with a plant biologist reassuring the anxious reporter, 'Don't worry. After all, our

California eucalyptus actually migrated here from Australia,' the play the piece got on the local six o'clock news made comparison with human immigration to the region hard to avoid. Southern Californians had, in any case all but grown up to the background noise of reports on local efforts to combat medfly infestations. These insects, too, were foreigners, and if they weren't stopped, the state agricultural authorities insisted, they would ruin California's crops. And so every year, sections of the Southland would be sprayed by crop dusters, in an eerie recapitulation (for those who were historically minded) of other national campaigns of eradication and interdiction. Despite repeated lawsuits brought by a coalition of environmental and citizens' groups, their case buttressed by the strong suspicion among many doctors that the pesticide being used, a compound called Malathion, was unlikely to interact with human lung tissue any more leniently than it did with the paint finishes on cars all over greater Los Angeles, the spraying went on. Perhaps the authorities are right, and California agriculture would be destroyed if the medflies were allowed to gain a foothold, but at the very least the linguistic congruences between the ways people talked about the medflies and that same language of invasion and contamination used in a somewhat different context about illegal immigration was startling. As for the alarmist reports of the colonies of South American soldier ants which, by 1990, were said to have reached Baja California, there the less said the better.

It was too easy to grow accustomed to the way white Angelenos would speak of aliens 'pouring' into the country, the hypertrophied rhetoric, at times grotesquely biblical in character, of 'floods', 'waves', and 'invasions'. And yet most peculiar of all, in a way, was that all this apocalyptic thinking was occurring in Los Angeles, precisely the place where people had for so long prided themselves on being beyond history, beyond ethnicity. But ready or not, all the grand and painful dramas of race, nation, and identity, dormant for almost half a century, were being resurrected. And many people were at least dimly aware that such an event could not have come at a worse time. Whatever its vices, the existence of a WASP ruling class that was so firmly in control – politically, culturally, and economically – at the turn of the century had ensured that when the great immigration from northeastern and southeastern Europe took place, there was a national culture for the new arrivals to aspire to. But precisely the Californianization of the United States over the course of the twentieth century had put paid to all that. In a country of individuals and their things, everything was up for grabs.

That was where, most of all, the new nativists who spoke of the sanctity of America's borders had got it wrong. The unsettling of the old American order had been capitalism's great work, an enterprise that had found its highest expression in the city of Los Angeles. In that system, the economy was supposed to expand indefinitely, just as the metropolis itself was destined to push its way not just to the mountains that ring the L.A. basin but across them into the desert, and north and south as well. And for the period in which growth had looked as if it would go on for ever, this Los Angelesization of the country had made sense. 'There is more to life than growing faster,' Ganchi once said, but for a long time L.A. appeared like a living refutation of his statement.

To its detractors, Los Angeles was the city where you 'got away' with everything; 'reality with a substitute teacher,' as the writer Ellis Weiner once quipped. Ronald Reagan's best scriptwriter, Peggy Noonan, echoed this view when, in her memoirs, she criticized her boss for reflecting 'what's dangerous about California – that life is so soft there, it's like moving through a lovely haze of warm gelatin.' In reality, what had been moving along so easily was not California but capitalism. The ease, the sense in which for several generations, it provided more people with more creature comforts, was merely the byproduct of its success. If people had been able to deny the harsher realities, it was because for all sorts of reasons the American economy had something of a free ride between the end of World War II and the end of the Vietnam War. Now, it turned out, that free ride was over and Americans would have to dance as fast as everyone else had been doing in the rest of the developed world.

For it turned out that the growth could not in fact go on for ever, that neither the environment nor the world economy were anywhere near as elastic as had been assumed. There were limits to credit, just as there were limits to the earth's ability to withstand the defilement of man. And just as the older residents of Southern California were waking up to these limitations on what, theretofore, they had conceived of as their birthright – wasn't that the American Dream? Wasn't that the promise of all those movies, and television shows, and ad campaigns? – along came the rest of the world, or, at least, a sizable chunk of it, anyway. And the irony was that in Mexico City, and Esfahan and Seoul, in Lima, Taipei, and San Salvador, they had seen those same movies. Dubbed, of course. And now, as the California of unbridled expansion was psyching itself up to confront its own contradictions, there was the rest of the world, clamoring for admission an alien nation before the gates of perhaps the only country in history that had genuinely believed that its dreams were unique and inviolable, and had surely never imagined the time would come when they would be unsettled by the dreary wake-up call of history and demography. The fact that, to so many Angelenos, this utopia had not been a fantasy but the daily experience of a good part of their lives made the transformation that was taking place all around them seem like the most terrible betrayal, and I found few takers for my suggestion that betrayals and reversals of fortune are, precisely, the usual currencies in which history deals. All fundamentalisms fear contamination by strangers, not least that fundamentalism called paradise. It was perhaps because he saw this that Christopher Isherwood once said that California was a tragic place, 'like Palestine, like every promised land'.

© David Rieff 1991

Opposite, VIRGIN OF GUADALUPE CANDLES, immigrant encampment next to the Santa Ana Freeway, downtown Los Angeles, 1989

Jazz

FUNERALS

PHOTOGRAPHS BY LEE FRIEDLANDER

Lee Friedlander started photographing the musicians of New Orleans in 1957, when, as he puts it, the music was 'still being played indigenously'. The following photographs, and **Whitney Balliett's** description of a trip he made there in 1966, are from Friedlander's book *The Jazz People of New Orleans*.

'Hello and good morning,' Dick Allen said on the telephone. I had written to Allen a few weeks before I went to New Orleans and he had agreed to shepherd me around. 'We're lucky,' he said, 'which isn't quite the right word under the circumstances – because I've just found out there's a funeral this afternoon in Walkertown, in Marrero. That's about eight miles out on the other side of the river, and there will be two bands – the Young Tuxedo and the Olympia. Betty Rankin, who is the associate curator at the Archive Museum now, is taking us out.'

On the other side of the river, we drove between low, woolly clouds and flat country anchored by shopping centers and small factories. 'The country funeral with brass bands is rapidly vanishing,' Allen said. 'The well-to-do and middle-class Negroes have begun to look down on it. They consider it Uncle Tom. It's too bad. There is no ritual like it anywhere in the world – dirge music on the way to the cemetery, and swinging music on the way back. They show death respect and then rejoice in life.'

Walkertown is a dirt-poor Negro hamlet. Its one-story wooden houses are set on stilts, and the front yards are shabby. There are almost no trees. The dusty white streets, made of crushed clamshells, are flanked by open drainage ditches with planks for bridges. Mrs Rankin pulled up near the Morning Star Baptist Church, a long wooden building with a mock-Spanish steeple. An enormous ear-trumpet loudspeaker was fastened to the front wall of the steeple, and air-conditioners jutted out of most of the windows.

Several musicians were milling around in front of the church. One of them strolled past and, seeing Allen, leaned into the car and said, 'Hey, you brought yourself! How you feeling?'

It began to rain, and a second musician appeared. It was Kid Thomas. 'Man, it rains at a funeral, it means it's washing away the dead man's sins. A really big sinner, it rains like hell.' He smiled, showing a lot of gold teeth.

The rain stopped, and we got out of the car. A thin female voice, singing a hymn, came out of the loudspeaker. A static-filled silence followed, and then a man spoke. A series of moans and screams grew louder and louder behind his words.

'The bereaved women generally try to outscream one another,' Mrs Rankin said. 'I once went to a funeral where the deceased had a legal and a non-legal wife, and they screamed at each other for fifteen minutes. It was quite a show.'

The church door opened, and two women in black and white, their faces wet and contorted, hobbled out on the arms of several men. A file of men wearing Odd Fellows' ceremonial aprons and neckpieces followed. The Young Tuxedo Band and the Olympia Band played a slow 'Just a Closer Walk with Thee'. Then the Olympia marched past the church and turned into Ames Boulevard, with the Young Tuxedo about fifty feet behind. A dozen Odd Fellows walked between them. The snare drum was muffled and the beat was slow. 'Saviour Lead Me', by the Olympia, was followed by the Young Tuxedo's 'What a Friend We Have in Jesus'. Dead, soft drumbeats separated the numbers. The second line ambled along quietly at one side of the road, and a long string of limousines nosed the Young Tuxedo. The procession moved between a housing development and a farmyard full of guinea hens, between a power station and a field of cows, and after a mile or so it halted at a wooden bridge over a deep ditch. On the other side, a dirt road disappeared into a patch of woods. The Young Tuxedo marched across the bridge, followed by the hearse, which moved cautiously, filling the bridge. The cemetery began on the left of the dirt road, and was a bedraggled sea of small stones, briars, wooden crosses, and long grass. Refuse had been dumped as fill on the other side of the road. A tunnel of trees dripped and whispered. The Young Tuxedo played 'Saviour Lead Me' at the grave, and after the service the mourners walked slowly back to the boulevard. The Young Tuxedo suddenly started 'When the Saints Go Marching In'. The second line materialized in front. The sun came out, burnishing one of the tubas. The Olympia began a fast 'Just a Closer Walk with Thee'. In the second line, a fat man dressed in a tight blue suit and a small fedora threw back his head, switched his hips, and strutted through a crowd of leaping, delighted children. The two tear-drenched women from the church danced arm in arm. An old woman flopped heavily in circles, like a turkey with an injured wing, and was joined by an old man, who pumped his knees and trembled his hands. The returning limousines roared past, leaving big white dust-devils. The Young Tuxedo played 'Bye and Bye'. The road was filled with dancers, and when the rain started again there were little screams.

We moved into Third Street and stopped in front of the house belonging to the head of the Odd Fellows. The old woman danced into a front yard across the street and onto the porch. Both bands, packed into a circle, played 'Lord, Lord, Lord'. It lasted five minutes. Twenty instruments rose and fell in broken, glorious waves. The rain let up, and the music

1 Club Memeers
2 Young Tuxedo Brass Band

Opposite

Johnny St. Cyr &
'Fess' Manetta

ended, stunning us all. The dancers ran down, and I could hear cars on Ames Boulevard. A thin middle-aged man in a cowboy hat said, 'That was my papa was buried today. Fifty years he was an Odd Fellow.'

Mrs Rankin and Allen walked back to the car. 'I don't believe I've been to a finer country funeral,' she said.

'I share your feelings,' Allen replied.

Not long after I got back to New York, I went to see Red Allen, who was born in New Orleans in 1908, and is one of the great jazz trumpeters. He told me what the funeral and parade I had just been to might have been like fifty years earlier: 'The brass bands generally had two trombones, three trumpets, a bass horn and a baritone horn, a peck horn, a clarinet, and two drummers. The trombones marched in front, so they wouldn't hit anybody in the back. The bass and baritone came next, then the clarinet and the peck horn, the trumpets, and then the drummers – bass drum on the left and snare drum to the right. The bass drummer played his drum and a cymbal attached to it, and the other drummer played snares. The two of them got a sound like a regular set of drums. The horn players needed strong embouchures. The roads were rough and if you stepped into a hole you had to hold on to that horn to not break your notes. Maybe that was the reason King Oliver never marched with the band but always next to it, on the sidewalk, where it was smoother. There were generally parades on Sundays, and of course when there was a decease and for special occasions, like housebuildings and the regular outings of the social clubs. I don't know how many social clubs there were – the Money Wasters, the Square Deals, the Bulls, the West Side Friends of Honor. You paid dues and when you passed your club paid for a band and for putting you away. The big men belonged to four or five clubs and they'd have four or five bands. My father had six when he passed. If you weren't a member of any club, they put a saucer on your chest while you lay in the front room and pretty soon there'd be enough for the proper arrangements. Each club had its own colors and its own banner. In parades, the two men who carried the banner got twenty-five cents apiece, and the man who carried the American flag got fifty cents. And each club had its own button – black on one side and its colors on the other. You'd wear the colors for the regular parades and the black for funerals. The men who played in the bands were stonemasons or slaters or plasterers and such, and their jobs would let them off for a funeral. These funerals went according to the Bible – sadness at birth and rejoicing at death. If the deceased belonged to several clubs, he'd generally stay on view in the front room for three or four days to give all his brothers time to pay their respects. If you were very sacred, you'd stay with the deceased some while, then you'd go through to the kitchen, where they'd have a bousin, which is a Creole term for a party. There would be gumbo and ham salad and burgundy and sangaree, a kind of punch.

'On funeral days, the club and the band assembled at the deceased's house and then they'd march to the church. The band played very slow, very slow. The snare was taken off on the snare drum, giving a kettle effect. When the deceased went by, everyone in the street would stop talking and moving and take off their hats and put them over their hearts, and then go back to what they were doing. While everyone was in the church, the musicians sometimes went to a saloon nearby, and it was my job when I was little to run from the church to the saloon when the service was over and get the musicians together. We'd march to the cemetery and the band would stand in the road and wait until the moans and cries went up, which meant that the preacher was saying, "Ashes to ashes, and dust to dust," and throwing the dirt on the coffin. Then the drums rolled like thunder and the band would break into a fast "Oh, Didn't He Ramble" and march back. On a wide avenue, when there was more than one band, the first band would split in half, one half lining up on one side of the avenue, and the other on the other side, and the band right behind would march between these lines. The bands would be playing different tunes. Then the second band would split open and the first one would form up again and march through them. You could tell by the applause of the onlookers who was best, and the winner would go a roundabout way to the house of the deceased and play up there on the gallery, really swinging, for ten or fifteen minutes, and then go inside and enjoy the bousin.

'Of course we played at dances, too. The men in the band would get three dollars apiece and the leader four and there was a dollar allowed for phone calls and such. And there were building parties. When a man decided to build himself a house it was like the pioneering days. The members of his club and his neighbors would all gather on a weekend on his plot – wives and children, too. The men would put down the foundation and get the frame up. There would be a few kegs of beer or some home brew – Sweet Lucy or Son Kick Your Mammy – and a band to play. They'd build and eat and build and drink and build and laugh and have a fine bousin. The man whose house was being put up would turn around next time a house had to be built and help with that. At Mardi Gras, musicians got scarce in New Orleans, and a week or so before, my father would hitch up a sulky and travel maybe a hundred miles into the country to round up musicians he'd heard or heard about. He took me when I got big enough. The roads were poor, and we never went too fast for fear the horse's legs might get stoved up or swollen. We'd stop and visit every few miles and spend the night with relatives or friends.'

Allen died just a year later, aged fifty-nine.

© Whitney Balliett 1992

CITY OF BOYS

BETH NUGENT

PHOTOGRAPHS BY THE DOUGLAS BROTHERS

—MY LITTLE SWEETHEART, SHE SAYS, BRINGING
HER FACE CLOSE ENOUGH FOR ME TO SEE THE
FINE NET OF LINES THAT CARVES HER FACE INTO
A WEATHERED STONE. —YOU LOVE ME, DON'T
YOU LITTLE SWEETHEART, LITTLE LAMB?

WHETHER OR NOT SHE LISTENS ANYMORE, I
AM NOT SURE, BUT I ALWAYS ANSWER YES; YES,

I always say, yes, I love you.

She is my mother, my father, my sister, brother, cousin, lover; she is everything I ever thought any one person needed in the world. She is everything but a boy.

—Boys, she tells me. —Boys will only break you.

I know this. I watch them on the street corners, huddled under their puddles of blue smoke. They are as nervous as insects, always some part of their bodies in useless, agitated motion, a foot tapping, a jaw clenching, a finger drawing circles against a thigh, eyes in restless programmed movement as they watch women pass — they look from breasts to face to legs to breasts. They are never still and they twitch and jump when I walk by, but still I want them. I want them in the back seats of their cars; I want them under the bridge where the river meets the rocks in a slick slide of stone; I want them in the back rows of theaters and under the bushes and benches in the park.

—Boys, she says. —Don't even think about boys. Boys would only make you do things you don't know how to do and things you'd never want to do if you knew what they were. I know, she says, —I know plenty about boys.

She is everything to me. She is not my mother, though I have allowed myself the luxury of sometimes believing myself her child. My mother is in Fairborn, Ohio, where she waits with my father for me to come home and marry a boy and become the woman into whom she still believes it is not too late for me to grow. Fairborn is a city full of boys and parking meters and the Air Force, but most of all it is a city full of my mother, and in my mind, she looms over it like a cloud of radioactive dust. If I return, it will be to her. She is not why I left, she is not why I am here; she is just one thing I left, like all the things that trail behind us when we go from place to place, from birth to birth, from becoming to becoming. She is just another bread crumb, just another mother in the long series of mothers that let you go to become the woman you have to become. But you are always coming back to them.

Where I live now is also a city full of boys, and, coming here, I passed through hundreds of cities and they were all full of boys.

—Boys, she tells me, —are uninteresting, and when they grow up, they become men and become even more uninteresting.

I know this too. I see how boys spend their days, either standing around or playing basketball or engaged in some irritating, persistent harangue, and I can draw my own conclusions as to what they talk about and as to the heights of which they are capable, and I see what they do all day, but still I want them.

The one time I pretended she was a boy, she knew it, because I closed my eyes, and I never close my eyes, and when I came, she slapped me hard.

—I'm not a boy, she said, —just you remember that. You know who I am and just remember that I love you and no boy could ever love you like I do.

Probably she is right. What boy could love with her slipping concentration? Probably no boy could ever achieve what she lets go with every day that comes between us, what she has lost in her long history of love.

What I do sometimes is slip out under her absent gaze.

—Where are you going, what are you going to do? she says, and, wallowing in the luxury of thinking myself a child, I answer: Nowhere. Nothing.

In their pure undirected, intoxicating meaninglessness, our conversations carry more significance than either of us is strong enough to bear, together or alone, and I drag it out into the streets today, a long weight trailing behind me, as I look for boys.

Today, I tell myself, is a perfect day for losing things, love and innocence, illusions and expectations; it is a day through which I will wander until I find the perfect boy.

Where we live, on the upper West Side, the streets are full of Puerto Rican men watching women. Carefully they examine each woman who passes, carefully they hold her with their eyes, as if they are somehow responsible for her continued existence on the street. Not a woman goes by untouched by the long leash of their looks. Ohh, Sssss, they say. Mira, mira, and when a woman looks they smile and hiss again through their shiny teeth. In their eyes are all the women they have watched walk by and cook and comb their black hair; all the women they have touched with their hands and all the women they have known live in their eyes and gleam out from within the dark. Their eyes are made only to see women on the streets.

Where we live, on West Eighty-third and Amsterdam, there are roaches and rats, but nothing matters as long as we're together, we say valiantly, longingly. Nothing matters, I say, stomping a roach, and nothing matters, she agrees, her eyes on a low-slung rat sidling by in the long hallway toward the little garbage room across from the door to our apartment. I told the super once that if he kept the garbage out on the street, perhaps the building would be less a home for vermin.

—What's vermin? he wanted to know.

Vermin, I told him, is rats and roaches and huge black beetles scrabbling at the base of the toilet when you turn on the light at night. Vermin is all the noises at night, all the clicking and scratching and scurrying through the darkness.

—No rats, he said. —Maybe a mouse or two, and maybe every now and then you'll see your roach eggs, but I keep this place clean.

Together we watched as a big brown-shelled roach tried to creep past us on the wall. Neither of us moved to kill it, but when it stopped and waved its antennae, he brought his big fist down in a hard slam against the wall. He didn't look at the dead roach, but I could hardly take my eyes off it, perfectly flattened, as though it had been steamrolled against the side of his hand.

—Maybe a roach here and there, he said, flicking the roach onto the floor without looking at it, —but I keep this place clean. Maybe if you had a man around the house, he said, trying to look past me into our apartment, —you wouldn't have so much trouble with vermins.

I pretended not to understand what he meant, and backed into the room. Rent control is not going to last for ever in New

York, and when it goes and all the Puerto Ricans have had to move to the Bronx, we will have to find jobs or hit the streets, but as long as we're together, as long as we have each other, somehow it will all be fine.

—We'll always have each other, won't we? she says, lighting a cigarette and checking to see how many are left in her pack.

—Yes, I always say, wondering if she's listening or just lost in a cigarette count. You'll always have me, I say. Unless, I think, unless you leave me, or unless I grow up to become the woman my mother still thinks is possible.

Today is a day full of boys. They are everywhere, and I watch each of them, boys on motorcycles, boys in cars, on bicycles, leaning against walls, walking; I watch them all to see which of them in this city of boys is mine.

I am not so young and she is not so old, but rent control is not going to last for ever, and someday I will be a woman. She wants, I tell myself, nothing more than me. Sometimes I think she must have been my mother, the way she loves me, but when I asked her if she were ever my mother, she touched my narrow breasts and said: Would your mother do that? and ran her tongue over my skin and said: Or that? Would your mother know what you want, sweetheart? I'm not your mother, she said, I stole you from a mattress downtown, just around the corner from where all the winos lie around in piss and wine and call for help and nobody listens. I saved you from that, she said. But I remember too clearly the trip out here, in the middle of a car full of people full of drugs, most of them, and I remember how she found me standing just outside the porn theater on Ninety-eighth and Broadway, and she slipped me right from under the gaze of about a hundred curious Puerto Ricans.

—Does your mother know where you are? she asked me.

I laughed and said my mother knew all she needed to know, and she said Come home with me. I have somebody I want you to meet. When she brought me home, she took me right over to a big man who lay on the couch watching television.

—Tito, this is Princess Grace, she said, and Tito raised his heavy head from the pillow to look me over.

—She don't look like no princess to me, was all he said, then he put his head back down and kept on watching his show.

I never thought much of Tito, and she never let him touch me, even though our apartment is only one room, and he was sick with wanting me. At night, after they'd finished with each other, she crept over to me in my corner and whispered in my ear, Sweetheart, you are my only one.

As Tito snored through the nights, we'd do it at least one more time than they had, and she would sigh and say —Little Sweetheart, you are the one I wanted all the time, even with all those other boys and girls who loved me, it was always you that I was looking for, you that I wanted.

This is the kind of talk that kills me; this is the kind of talk that won me, in addition to the fact that she took me in from the hard streets full of boys and cops and taxicabs, and everywhere I looked the hard eyes of innocence turned.

That first time with her I felt as though my mother were curled up inside my own body giving birth to me; each time she let me go, I made my way back inside her.

The long car pulls up to the sidewalk and I bend to see if it has boys in it. It is full of them, so I say: —Hey, can I have a ride?

—Hey, they say. —Hey, the lady wants a ride. Where to? they ask.

—Oh, I say. —Wherever. I look to see where they are heading. —Uptown, I say, and the door swings open, so I slide in. The oldest boy is probably sixteen and just got his driver's license, and he is driving his mother's car, a big Buick or Chevrolet or Monte Carlo — a mother's car. Each of the boys is different, but they are all exactly alike in the way that boys are, and right away I pick the one I want. He's the one who does not look at me, and he's the oldest, only a couple of years younger than I, and it is his mother's car we are in.

—How about a party? the boys say. —We know a good party uptown.

—Let's just see, I say. —Let's just ride uptown and see.

Sometimes I wake up to see her leaning on her thin knees against the wall that is stripped down to expose the rough brick beneath the plaster. I dream that she prays to keep me, but I am afraid that it is something else she prays for, a beginning, or an end, or something I don't know about. She came to bed once and lay her face against my breast, and I felt the imprint of the brick in the tender skin of her forehead.

She herself is not particularly religious, although the apartment is littered with the scraps of saints — holy relics of one sort or another: a strand of hair from the Christ child, a bit of fingernail from Saint Paul, a shred of the Virgin's robe. They are left over from Tito, who collected holy relics the way some people collect lucky pennies or matchbooks, as a hedge against some inarticulated sense of disaster. They are just clutter here, though, in this small apartment where we live, and I suggested to her once that we throw them out. She picked up a piece of dried weed from Gethsemane and said, —I don't think they're ours to throw out. Tito found them and if we got rid of them, who knows what might happen to Tito. Maybe they work, is what I mean, she said. —And besides, I don't think it's spiritually economical to be a skeptic about absolutely everything.

When Tito left, his relics abandoned for some new hope, she was depressed for a day or two, but said finally that it really was the best for everybody, especially for the two of us, the single reality to which our lives have been refined. Tito said he was getting sick of watching two dykes moon over each other all the time, though I think he was just angry because she wouldn't let him touch me. I was all for it, I wanted him to touch me. That's what I came to this city for: to have someone like Tito touch me, someone to whom touching is all the reality of being, someone who doesn't do it in basements and thinks he has to marry you, someone who does it and doesn't think about the glory of love. But she wouldn't have it; she said if he ever touched me, she would send me back to the Ninety-eighth Street porn theater and let the Puerto Ricans make refried beans out of me, and as for Tito, he could go back to Rosa, his wife in Queens, and go back to work lugging papers for the *Daily News* and ride the subway every day and go home and listen to Rosa talk on the phone all night, instead of hanging out on street corners and playing cards with the men outside the schoolyard, like he did now. Because, she said, because she was paying the rent, and as long as rent control lasted in New York, she would continue to pay the rent, and she could live quite happily and satisfactorily by herself until she found the right sort of roommate; one, she said, fingering the shiny satin of Tito's shirt, who paid the rent.

So Tito kept his distance and kept us both sick with his desire, and when she finally stopped sleeping with him and joined me on the mattress on the floor, even Tito could see that it wasn't going to be long before we'd be taking the bed and he would have to move to the floor. To save himself from that, he said one day that he guessed he was something of a fifth wheel around the joint, huh? and he'd found a nice Puerto Rican family that needed a man around the house and he supposed he'd just move in with them. I think he was only trying to save face, though, because one day when she was out buying cigarettes, he roused himself from the couch and away from the television to say to me —You know, she was married before, you know.

—I know that, I said. —I know all about that.

How she pays the rent is with alimony that still comes in from her marriage and I know all about that and Tito wasn't telling me anything that I didn't know, so I looked back at the magazine I was reading and waited for him to go back to the television. He kept looking at me, so I got up to look out the window to see if I could see her coming back and if she had anything for me.

—What I'm trying to say, he said, —what I'm trying to tell you is that you're not the only one. You're not. I was the only one, too, the one she was always looking for. I was the one before you, and you're just the one before someone else.

I could see her rounding the corner from Ninety-sixth and Broadway, and could see that she had something in a bag for me, doughnuts or cookies. I said nothing, only looked out the window and counted the steps she took toward our building. She was leaning forward and listing slightly toward the wall, so I guessed that she must have had a few drinks in the bar where she always buys her cigarettes. When I could hear her key turning in the lock to the street door, I went to open our door for her and Tito reached out and grabbed me by the arm. —Listen, he said. —You just listen. Nobody is ever the only one for nobody. Don't kid yourself.

I pulled away and opened the door for her. When she came in, cold skin and wet, I put my face in her hair and breathed in the smell of gin and cigarettes, and all the meaning of my life.

The next day Tito left, but he didn't go far, because I still see him hanging out on street corners. Now all the women he has known are in his eyes, but mostly there is her, and when he looks at me, I cannot bear to see her lost in the dark there. Whenever I pass him, I always smile.

—Hey Tiiiiiiito, I say. —Mira mira, huh? And all his friends laugh, while Tito tries to look as though this is something he's planned himself, as though he has somehow elicited this remark from me.

I suppose one day Tito will use the key he forgot to leave behind to sneak in and cover me with his flagging desire, his fading regrets, and his disappointments, and she will move on then, away from me; but rent control will not last for ever in New York, and I cannot think ahead to the beginnings and the ends for which she prays.

The boys in the car lean against one another and leer and twitch like tormented insects, exchanging glances that they think are far too subtle for me to understand, but I have come too far looking for too much to miss any of it. We drive too fast up Riverside, so that it's no time at all before the nice neighborhoods become slums full of women in windows, with colorful clothing slung over fire escapes, and like a thick haze hanging over the city, the bright noise of salsa music. Like the sound of crickets threading through the Ohio summer nights, it sets the terms for everything.

—So, one of them says, —so where are you going, anyways?

—Well, I say. —Well, I was thinking about going to the Bronx Botanical Gardens.

The Bronx Botanical Gardens is no place I'd ever really want to go, but I feel it's important to maintain, at least in their eyes, some illusion of destination. If I was a bit more sure of myself, I'd suggest that we take the ferry over to Staten Island and do it in the park there. Then I could think of her.

When we went to Staten Island, it was cold and gray and windy; we got there and realized that there was nothing really that we wanted to see, that being in Staten Island was really not all that different from being in Manhattan. —Or anywhere, she said, looking down a street into a corridor of rundown clothing stores and insurance offices. It was Sunday, so everything was closed up tight and no one was on the street. Finally we found a coffee shop near the ferry station, where we drank Cokes and coffee, and she smoked cigarettes, while we waited for the boat to leave.

—Lezzes, the counterman said to another man sitting at the counter eating a doughnut. —What do you want to bet they're lezzes?

The man eating the doughnut turned and looked us over.

—They're not so hot anyways, he said. —No big waste.

She smiled and held her hand to my face for a second; the smoke from her cigarette drifted past my eyes into my hair. —What a moment, she said, —to remember.

On the way back, I watched the wind whip her face all out of any shape I knew, and when I caught the eyes of some boys on the ferry, she said, not looking at me, not taking her eyes from the concrete ripples of the robe at the feet of the Statue of Liberty just on our left, —What you do is your own business, but don't expect me to love you for ever if you do things like this. I'm not, she said, turning to look me full in the face, —your mother, you know. All I am is your lover, and nothing lasts for ever.

When we got off the ferry, I said: —I don't expect you to love

me for ever, and she said I was being promiscuous and quarrelsome, and she lit a cigarette as she walked down into the subway station. I watched her as she walked, and it seemed to me to be the first time I had ever seen her back, walking away from me, trailing a long blue string of smoke.

Something is going on with the boys, something has changed in the set of their faces, the way they hold their cigarettes, the way they nudge each other. Something changes when the light begins to fade and one of them says to me: —We have a clubhouse uptown, want to come there with us?

—What kind of club, I ask, —what do you do there?

—We drink whisky, they say, —and take drugs and watch television. My boy, the one I have picked out of this whole city of boys, stares out the window, chewing at a toothpick he's got wedged somewhere in the depths of his jaw, and runs his finger over the slick plastic of the steering wheel. I can tell by his refusal to ask that he wants me to come. This, I suppose, is how to get to the center of boys, to go to their club. Boys are like pack creatures, and they always form clubs; it's as though they cannot help themselves. It's the single law of human nature that I have observed in my limited exposure to the world, that plays and plays and replays itself out with simple mindless consistency: where there are boys, there are clubs, and anywhere there is a club, it is bound to be full of boys, looking for the good times to be had just by being boys.

—Can I join? I ask. This is what I will take back to her, cigarettes and a boy's club. This will keep her for me for ever: that I have gone to the center of boys and have come back to her.

—Well, they say, and smirk and grin and scratch at themselves. —Well, there's an initiation.

The oldest of the boys is younger than I, and yet, like boys everywhere, they all think that I don't know nearly so much as they do, as if being a woman somehow short circuits my capacity for input. They have a language that they think only boys can understand, but understanding their language is the key to my success, so I smile and say: —I will not fuck you all, separately or together.

My boy looks over at me and permits himself a cool half-smile, and I am irritated that he now holds me in higher regard because I can speak a language that any idiot could learn.

Between us there are no small moments; we do not speak at all or we speak everything. Heat bills and toothpaste and dinner and all the dailiness of living are given no language in our time together. I realize that this kind of intensity cannot be sustained over a long period of time and that every small absence in our days signals an end between us. She tells me that I must never leave her, but what I know is that someday she will leave me with a fistful of marriage money to pay the rent as long as rent control lasts in New York, and I will see her wandering down the streets, see her in the arms of another, and I say to her sometimes late at night when she blows smoke rings at my breasts: Don't leave me. Don't ever ever leave me.

—Life, she always says to me, —is one long leave-taking. Don't kid yourself, she says. —Kid, and laughs. —Anyways, you are my little sweetheart, and how could I ever leave you, and how could I leave this — soft touch on my skin — and this, and this.

She knows this kills me every time.

Their clubhouse is dirty and disorganized and everywhere there are mattresses and empty beer bottles and bags from McDonald's, and skittering through all of this mess are more roaches than I thought could exist in a single place, more roaches than there are boys in this city, more roaches than there are moments of love in this world.

The boys walk importantly in. This is their club; they are New York City boys and they take drugs and they have a club, and I watch as they scatter around and sit on mattresses and flip on the television. I hang back in the doorway and reach out to snag the corner of the jacket my boy is wearing. He turns to me without interest.

—How about some air? I say.

—Let me just get high first, he says, and he walks over to a chair and sits down and pulls out his works and cooks up his dope and ties up his arm and spends a good two minutes searching out a vein to pop. All over his hands and arms and probably his legs and feet and stomach are signs of collapse and ruin, as if his body has been created for a single purpose, and he has spent a busy and productive life systematically mining it for good places to fix.

I watch him do this while the other boys do their dope or roll their joints or pop their pills, and he offers me some. I say no, I'd rather keep a clear head, and how about some air?

I don't want him to hit a nod before any of it's even happened, but this is my experience with junkies, that they exit right out of every situation before it's even become a situation.

—Let's take the car, he says.

You are my sweetheart, she says, and if you leave me, you will spend all your life coming back to me. With her tongue and her words and the quiet movement of her hand over my skin, she has drawn for me all the limits of my life, and of my love. It is the one love that has created me and will contain me, and if she left me I'd be lonely, and I'd rather sleep in the streets with her hand between my legs for ever than be lonely.

In the car, the boy slides his hand between my legs and then puts it on the steering wheel. A chill in the air, empty streets, and it's late. Every second takes me further into the night away from her; every second sends me home. We drive to Inwood Park, and climb the fence so that we are only a few feet away from the Hudson.

—This is nothing like Ohio, I say to him, and he lights a cigarette.

—Where's Ohio?

—Don't you go to school? I ask him. —Don't you take geography?

—I know what I need to know, he says, and reaches over to unbutton my blouse. The thing about junkies is that they know they don't have much time, and the thing about boys is that they know how not to waste it.

—This is very romantic, I say, as his fingers hit my nipples like a piece of ice. —Do you come here often?

What I like about this boy is that he just puts it right in. He just puts it in as though he does this all the time, as though he doesn't usually have to slide it through his fingers, or between his friends' rough lips; he just puts it in and comes like wet soap shooting out of a fist, and this is what I wanted. This is what I wanted, I say to myself as I watch the Hudson rolling brownly by over his shoulder. This is what I wanted, but all I think about is the way it is with us; this is what I wanted, but all I see is her face floating down the river, her eyes like pieces of moonlight caught in the water.

What I think is true doesn't matter anymore; what I think is false doesn't matter anymore. What I think at all doesn't matter anymore, because there is only her; like an image laid over my mind, she is superimposed on every thought I have. She sits by the window and looks out onto the street as though she is waiting for something, waiting for rent control to end, or waiting for something else to begin. She sits by the window waiting for something, and pulls a long string through her fingers. In the light from the window, I can see each of the bones in her hand; they make a delicate pattern that fades into the flesh and bone of her wrist.

—Don't ever change, I say to her. —Don't ever ever change.

She smiles and lets the string dangle from her hand.

—Nothing ever stays the same, she says. —You're old enough to know that aren't you, sweetheart? Permanence, she says, —is nothing more than a desire for things to stay the same.

I know this.

—Life is hard for me, the boy says. —What am I going to do with my life? I just hang around all day or drive my mother's car. Life is so hard. Everything will always be the same for me here in this city. It's going to eat me up and spit me out and I might as well never have been born. He looks poetically out over the river.

—I wanted a boy, I say, —not a poet.

—I'm not a poet, he says. —I'm just a junkie, and you're nothing but a slut. You can get yourself home tonight.

I say nothing and watch the Hudson roll by.

—I'm sorry, he says. —So what? So I'm a junkie and you're a slut, so what. Nothing ever changes. Besides, he says, —my teacher wants me to be a track star because I can run faster than anyone else in gym class. That's what he says.

—Well, that sounds like a promising career, I say, although I can imagine the teacher in his baggy sweatpants, his excitement rising as he stares at my boy and suggests after-school workouts. —Why don't you do that?

—I'd have to give up smoking, he says. —And dope.

Together we watch the river, and finally he says: —Well. It's about time I was getting my mother's car home.

—This is it? I ask him.

—What were you expecting? he says. —I'm only a junkie. In two years I probably won't even be able to get it up anymore.

—Look, I say, coming in and walking over to where she sits by the window. —Look. I am a marked woman. There is blood between my legs and it isn't yours.

She looks at me, then looks back at what she was doing before I came in, blowing smoke rings that flatten against the dirty window. —Did you bring me some cigarettes? she asks, putting hers out in the ashtray that rests on the windowsill.

—A marked woman, I say. —Can't you see the blood?

—I can't see anything, she says, —and I won't look until I have a cigarette.

I give her the cigarettes I bought earlier. Even in the midst of becoming a woman, I have remembered the small things that please her. She lights one and inhales the smoke, then lets it slowly out through her nose and her mouth at the same time. She knows this kills me.

—Don't you see it? I ask.

—I don't see anything, she says. —I don't see why you had to do this. She gets up and says, —I'm going to bed now. I've been up all day and all night and I'm tired and I want to go to sleep before the sun comes up.

—I am a marked woman, I say, lying beside her. —Don't you feel it?

—I don't feel anything, she says, but she holds me, and together we wait patiently for the light. She is everything to me. In the stiff morning before the full gloom of city light falls on us, I turn to her face full of shadows.

—I am a marked woman, I say. —I am.

—Quiet, she says, and puts her dark hand gently over my mouth, then moves it over my throat onto the rise of my chest. Across town, no one notices when she does this. Nothing is changed anywhere when she does this.

—Quiet, she says again. She presses her hand against my heart, and touches her face to mine and takes me with her into the motherless turning night. All moments stop here; this is the first and the last, and the only flesh is hers, the only touch her hand. Nothing else is, and together we turn under the stroke of the moon and the hiss of the stars; she is everything I will become and together we become every memory that has ever been known.

© Beth Nugent 1992

MICHAEL

ORMEROD

In August 1991, Michael Ormerod was killed in a road accident while photographing in Arizona. The cover photograph, the sequence which follows it, and some of the other images in this magazine are his.

Michael was born in Hyde, Cheshire, in 1947. After studying economics at Hull University, and photography at Trent Polytechnic, he ran a freelance photography business for many years, taught at Newcastle College, and made several trips to America, a country which became the main focus of his private work.

His relationship with America was complicated: like many photographers before him he was drawn by the light and space of the landscape, but he was also interested in the imposed fakeness he found there, a strange juxtaposition of the beautiful and the ugly. Many of his images suggest a hidden sense of menace and corruption, others are sympathetic portraits of people who display a knowingness and a wounded acceptance of their fate. Increasingly, Michael used his camera to describe inbetween places – the outskirts of towns which fringe the plains, the sides of roads – places where the landscape fights a silent battle with the man-made, where the forces of nature collide with the artificially banal. His photographs – many of which will be collected together in a book later this year – are a lasting testament to the journey America has travelled.

BOHUMIL HRABAL

THE WHITE HORSE

PHOTOGRAPH BY THE DOUGLAS BROTHERS

In this letter to an American friend, Bohumil Hrabal describes a recent trip he made to New York, a city that just wouldn't stay still for him . . .

Dear Dubenka,

So, here I am, in New York. I, son of Manhattan now, I Bohumil Hrabal, I cosmos of Prague-Liben, here I am, to pay my respects to Walt Whitman, who went about in a wheelchair at the end of his life, and still managed to teach that young man who pushed the royal poetic throne how to write poetry. Here I am, I've arrived from Washington, the capital, whose streets radiate off through the suburbs into the countryside, into the valleys of leafy trees, where brooks gurgle and felled tree-trunks lie across them so that everyone may see what the end looks like, not only of trees, but of all things. Now I'm in New York and I've been to the Bowery, and a bit further on to the main avenue, with its Banks of all Banks. It's a fantastic place, this city, where they show children who won't study how they'll end up like drunks dying on the street . . . and right next door the capital deposits of the Contented States . . . And here, Dubenka, I sailed round the Hudson strait and river with Susanna . . . it was misty, and the skyscrapers towered, covered waist-high in that tender mist, and our boat followed the line of the shore, and once again . . . how lovely those skyscrapers are, how breathtaking in their picaresque assemblage, and above the mist the office lights shining, a tremendous sight, those lights up there, almost where the sky begins! And another tremendous sight, along the shoreline there's a wire fence, a kind of belt all around Manhattan, a zone at least five or ten metres wide, where everything the city no longer requires glitters, as though it had all been put there on purpose by Kurt Schwitters, as though he was assisted by Robert Rauschenberg . . . and in that confusion of dead and discarded things rats slip and slither with slimy bellies . . . and the boys have an Eldorado there amongst the bushes and brushwood, that is their kingdom . . . theirs, but mine also, for as a boy I too loved all those dells and rubbish dumps at the back of St Vojtech's Church, where they carted off everything that people didn't want, had no use for any more, that had gone out of fashion . . . and died . . . And out on the avenues and streets, what lovely limousines passing by with ladies' knees on the back seats, what beauty, those American automobiles and their drivers, driving not by the highway code, but eyeball to eyeball, sharp

eyes decisive at the crossroads, crossroads just glittering with sharp eyes, the driver only carrying on along the main avenue when he detects assent in the eyes of the person entering from the sideroad . . . and out in the suburbs, what beauty, Dubenka, graveyards of motorcars, flattened automobiles that have served their time, grown obsolete, antiquated, gone out of fashion . . . Of course it's not just New York, every city in the world displays this juxtaposition of life and death, the maternity hospital and the funeral parlour . . . but here in New York this rhythm of life and death just hits you right between the eyes . . . here come elegant men and beautiful women, and down at knee level the eyes of those who beg, holding out their empty tins, it doesn't matter whether it's a woman sitting there or a man, white or black, each receives his small coin, and when the nickels have piled up to a certain point, the beggars get up and go to their own drinking den in their own street, and when they've drunk whatever they begged, they go back to where they sat before . . . It's a tremendous city, Dubenka, with tremendous collections of modern art and any old art, Dubenka, the staff in those museums wear a lovely blue uniform, just like the one I had as a dispatcher on the railways – in the summer I had a blue lustre jacket too – and what's more, all the staff have patent leather shoes, and mostly they're black women, who particularly watch their appearance . . . so Dubenka, I'm beside myself with this city, I'm not so bothered now about my lecture at Columbia, or Harcourt Brace Jovanovich bringing out my book *I Served the King of England* . . . I was moved to find Susanna and I were housed in a Presbyterian Methodist hotel, just a little up from the mouth of the Hudson river, where all that Robert Rauschenberg and Kurt Schwitters stuff lies on the shore, and that little hotel of ours in Greenwich Village, now that, Dubenka, is the most marvellous thing! Three days I spent visiting a small pub with Dutch beer on tap, for three days I couldn't get enough of the sight of those beautiful, dead-beat, smiling black girls, serving food and beer with big, fixed, V-like smiles, smiling all the time, as if they wanted me to marry them. It was lovely, Dubenka, in that little pub . . . I didn't even care about Susanna yelling at me every day at the publisher's or in the hotel . . . To hell with you, you and that Dubenka of yours, she's rung me up at the hotel again, she's phoned the administration at Brace Jovanovich to ask if we've arrived, if Mr Hrabal is feeling any better yet, and whether I'm looking after you properly . . . And you know, Dubenka, I admit it to you, repentantly, I did start looking after myself, and since the lowest death rate is found in public houses, I sat as much as I could in The White Horse tavern . . . and it was three days before I stopped looking at those girls' knees, those students who come in, throw off their coats, and sit and study with their lovely legs neatly crossed . . . but on the third day I discovered I was sitting at the window where Dylan Thomas used to sit, I saw his portrait in the corner, in oils, with a red nose, which suited him though, but of course with a drunkard everything goes . . . And then, there opposite was a polished bronze plaque, and on it the words, as Susanna translated them for me: If any of you talk of childhood, be quick, if you're slow, I'll interrupt and talk of my own, I, Dylan Thomas . . . And then another plaque, which Susanna didn't need to translate for me: RICHARD BURTON.

So there I sat, Dubenka, in The White Horse, with these black girls serving food and beer, above me they had a little ash-tray, and in it a cigarette, and as they swept past me they each just had time to take a drag, and they brushed a breast right up against my eye, just like long ago in The Golden Tiger, with Vera and Vlasta, properly brought-up barmaids in those days, and they too, before they laid the fresh beers on the tray, they rubbed a breast against my eyebrows, and I, Dubenka, then as now in The White Horse, I purred with ecstacy. So there I sat, meditatively, the black girls taking their intermittent puffs, and me sitting right where Dylan Thomas used to sit, until the drinking gave him delirium tremens and he died three days later in the St Vincent Hospital in New York . . .

Then came the real thunderbolt, Dubenka. Andy Warhol! That exhibition for which people stood in procession as if for a basketball match, so many people who all wanted to see what I'd too come for . . . Andy Warhol, the man who reached that height of emptiness and everydayness, who said it to everyone . . . What is tremendous about this country is that the richest in America can consume the same as the poorest. You can watch TV and drink Coca-Cola, you see the President drinking Coca-Cola, Liz Taylor drinks Coca-Cola too, and so can you . . . And I'm proud, Dubenka, that his parents came from Miková, from over near Medzilaborce, Andy Warhol's eyes are the eyes of Ruthenians and their melancholy, the eyes of peasant *muzhiks*, who drink out of despair at how short life is, and how a poor man has nothing except his honour . . . Dubenka, when it was our turn, we went into the huge foyer of the Museum of Modern Art, and there were several hundred cows with halters, several hundred cows adorning the walls like wallpaper, and at once I realised, before the Campbell's Soup there had to be these cows and their meat . . . and then, what we saw later, it was all familiar, all of it we had admired before, but we'd never attached such importance to it . . . till Andy came along with all those Liz Taylors, and all those Jackies, and all those dollar bills and 100-dollar bills, and electric chairs, in short, everything that surrounds us in this city, but it was only when Andy Warhol enlarged all his Polaroids with his Siebdruck technique, by silkscreening to two metres and more, only then did it all really tell us what draws us in human misfortune and beauty, in those champions of film and theatre and sport and public life . . . and discarded things and people, all that stuff we cannot tear our eyes away from, all those newspapers and news reports and posters, and so Andy Warhol caught us in the trap of our own making, so he gave art a whole extra dimension . . .

And then it was my birthday, and Hanka arrived from Palestine, that Jewish lass who, after my lecture at Columbia, offered to take me out for a birthday treat, invited me to a posh fish restaurant right down by Pier 17, where the boats leave for their trips round Manhattan. I asked, Dubenka, to be allowed to celebrate my three-quarters of a century at The White Horse, saying I had Dylan Thomas's table there, and that they were all invited . . . But, *asa chutzpah*, Hanka said we'd go to the fish restaurant and have a real surprise . . . and it was, Dubenka, it was, they had food all right, but no licence for beer, apparently it was the custom for visitors to bring their own . . . so Hanka brought along some Sappora beer in white bottles looking like milk, but it was worse than that, it was warm . . . and so I celebrated my three-quarters of a century with warm flat beer . . . and we ate à la carte all the best restaurant nosh, but what was the good of that, when over at The White Horse they had black waitresses and cold Dutch Heineken beer on tap . . . beer that tasted a bit like our own Popovice Bock . . . That was some surprise, Dubenka, it really was . . .

And on Saturday afternoon, before the lecture I was to give at the Sokol Hall, Mrs Jovanovich offered to take us wherever we liked . . . Now, back in Washington at Arnost Lustig's flat I'd already seen *The Unbearable Lightness of Being* . . . that film about sex ruling the world, then all of a sudden, smack bang! the Russians arrive in Prague, filmed by the Czech director Jan Nemec . . . so I wanted to see Kundera's film again, just for five minutes . . . or else, since Arnost and I had been going every day to hire one of Chaplin's films . . . *City Lights* and *The Gold Rush* and *Monsieur Verdoux* and *A King in New York*, we only missed *The Circus*, which they didn't have it in stock . . . so Mrs Jovanovich found out that *The Circus* was playing in some street near the Sokol Hall, and off we went in a taxi . . . only, after Mrs Jovanovich had leant forward into the box-office, she turned back and said with a smile . . . It's not playing today, there are seventeen Russian directors here, and they're going to have a discussion and show their films . . . and so instead Mrs Jovanovich took us to this place where they settle film contracts, and where New York artists meet, to Bob & Kenn's . . . and it was dark in there, but TV sets shone from the walls, and a softly-lit billiard table glowed greenly, and lovers sat there, and customers like us, eating . . . but everyone was staring at one of those screens, the basketball was on, and basketball for Americans is the highest, it's their own sporting pop-art . . . one basketballer, Jordan was his name, was playing his farewell match, and as a going-away present his fellow players and pals had bought him the most expensive English car, a Rolls Royce . . . That was quite a man, Dubenka, that was some player! He was from Washington and he scored a different way from all the others. Each time he magically caught the ball, which kind of hesitated in his pink palms for a bit, then he went round his opponents with his bent smooth-shaven head, and suddenly he thrust up those hands, and that leap – and the ball just swung into the net . . . Everyone was entranced by that black player Jordan, Susanna said, he always scored more than half the points in any match . . . And so we swapped *The Circus* and Soviet film directors for Jordan's last match at Bob & Kenn's . . .

And also, Dubenka, I was meant to meet Philip Roth, who had captivated me and made me hate my own writing with his book *The Ghost Writer* . . . but when we got to the office there was a note saying Mr Roth was sorry, he'd buzzed off some place . . . And also, one day Susanna and I went to visit Susan Sontag, that finest contemporary woman and writer, famous for her book about cancer . . . We went down from the street, into a basement, and there was a door and a handle, offered like a handshake, then a passage, and then a room just like mine in Kersko, and when the lady who led us down the passage turned, I saw it was she, Susan Sontag herself, who wrote that book about cancer, and wrote another book on AIDS. She invited Susanna and me to sit down, and then she sat down opposite us, a giantess with lovely eyes and a mane of hair with a silver streak at the front . . . we were quiet for a moment, then she asked me how the journey was, and whether we wanted coffee or tea . . . and she smiled and said, that book of hers, which I'd just praised, had actually been inspired by Prague – her father, when she was a girl, had made her read Karel Capek's play *The White Plague*, and she'd gone on reading it with keen interest, so actually her inspiration came from Central Europe . . . and she had deep eyes, and while Susanna interpreted what Susan Sontag was saying about the new book she was working on, I saw this lady was like the epigraph to *The Waste Land* . . . I saw the Cumaean Sibyl with my own eyes. She hung in a bottle, and when the boys asked her: Sibyl, what do you want? she replied: I want to die. Thus T. S. Eliot prefaced his *Waste Land* . . . And so I sat there with this lady, simple and wise and sad, our conversation floated in Central Europe, she knew the crossroads of linguistic consciousness, she knew that great literature can only arise in this manner, just like Emanuel Frynta taught me by the way . . . She also knew Arnost Lustig and his novels of Jewish suffering in Theresienstadt, she knew his story too, and I told her Lustig and I had been in Washington together, we'd seen nearly all of Charlie Chaplin's films, and Franz Kafka was an admirer of Chaplin too, he said of him something like this: From his eyes there gushes the ardour of despair at the immutable lot of ordinary folk below, who still never capitulate . . . And I told her that waiting for Lustig in Prague was the royal crown of David,

the crown which I had saved when the workmen demolished the altar of the Liben synagogue and then traded for a metre length of beer, that's eleven glasses of Pilsner . . . Arnost was going to send his sister over to bring it back for him, that crown which was his for the sake of Theresienstadt . . . And then we began discussing how in America there's an influx of literature and art in general from Eastern Europe. And I said, when we had the publisher's party for my book *I Served the King of England*, at Mrs Brace Jovanovich's, my translator Paul Wilson said Leslie Fiedler had called the period of the sixties to the eighties Post-modern . . . but he reckoned, as a translator expelled from Prague for playing with the group Plastic People, if you strike off the P, that tells you now what it is . . . not Post-modern but *Ost*-Modern, *East*-Modern. And Susan Sontag said, the way Mike Heim had translated my *Too Loud a Solitude*, she thanked me for it, she reckoned it would be one of the twenty books of the twentieth century. Michael Heim, Hungarian with Gypsy blood by the way, so he's East-Modern too.

And so it was, Dubenka, that while in New York we didn't bother too much about lectures at Columbia and when I wasn't sitting in The White Horse I amused myself with those images of the streets and avenue, and now I sat at Susan Sontag's, and together we played a kind of literary ping-pong, we outbid each other, outdid each other with names of writers and artists from the East . . . and Susan said: Marc Chagall . . . and I said Igor Stravinsky . . . and she said Singer . . . and I said Malamud, appending a title I love: *Idiots First* . . . and she said Philip Roth . . . and I said Josef Roth, *The Capuchin Crypt* . . . and she said Franz Kafka . . . and I replied Gustav Mahler . . . and she said Sigmund Freud . . . and I replied Walesa along with that new saint, Popieluszo . . . and she said Wojtyla, Pope John Paul II . . . and I raised my hand, and Susanna interpreted . . . last year the West German magazine *Spiegel* published a bestseller list . . . first place Mikhail Gorbachev . . . second by a narrow margin me . . . and Ernest Hemingway an honourable seventeenth . . . And we drank coffee, and a wintry sun emerged, the fluttering snow slanted down, and Dubenka, I must tell you this now, I was so cold here, Susanna had to buy some long johns, pants with sleeves as they jokingly call them in Prague . . . it still felt like winter even though the buds were swollen with spring . . . and we rejoiced that, indeed, all you did was strike off the P, and miraculously *Post*-Modern became *Ost*-Modern . . . and then I clasped my head and exclaimed . . . but we forgot about that other *Ost*-Modern . . . Andy Warhol! . . . Dubenka, Andy Warhol, a pale man with a silver wig, he that was born via his parents from over by Medzilaborce, just so that he could hold up a mirror to this city, and this society, he who studied art history, sociology and psychology, he who began, Dubenka, as an illustrator and an advertising and theatrical graphic artist, who started out with huge comic-strip canvases, and during the seventies magnified those idols of American life, Jackie Kennedy and Marilyn Monroe and Elvis Presley . . . and the 129 dead in a crashed jet! and that overturned car with five dead, and the girl's head hanging face upwards . . . and that sole of a man's boot in the tread of a huge truck . . . Dubenka, Andy Warhol, surrounded by beauties, even though he didn't believe in love, accompanied by guardian angels, Marisa Berenson and Lauren Hutton, beauties I dream of from the photographs of Andy's court photographer Christopher Makos, and Baryshnikov, the Russian ballet dancer in DJ and bow-tie, that's Andy's Archangel Gabriel, photographed with him at a show, Warhol, pale and wan, shot at in the year 1968 by that spitfire spurned in love, Valerie Solanas, who probably adored him, just as Mary Magdalene adored Christ, so that Andy could say, sex was too much of an effort, Andy, he who could unite the highest with the lowest, who could take photographs with a cheap Polaroid which looked as if they were done with the most expensive equipment . . . but especially he with the eyes of Christ, he who, when his sister used to visit, sang hymns with her from way back there in Medzilaborce, the man I specially came to see, and whose five-kilo-weight catalogue I bought, but then learnt off by heart, so that I could leave it behind for Mrs Meda Mladek who I stayed with in Washington, where I not only set fire to the pillows in my drunkenness, but also left bloodstains on the bed . . .

Then, in that Castle of New York, which contains the whole of world art in a nutshell, like a kind of child's concertina book for all who study the origins of art, I remember two more pictures . . . The tapestry of a unicorn, white and standing on a tiny islet, surrounded by a little gurgling stream, a unicorn with a white mane and skin, and lovely sad eyes filled with Eros . . . because only a virgin may speak to it, a young maiden who can give birth without ejaculation, like the Virgin Mary . . . and that young woman is on the other tapestry, only she is allowed, and has the power, to speak to the unicorn, who, however, is alone in the centre of the Paradise Garden . . . and then I remember another picture, the unicorn's no longer in that oval Paradise Garden, he's running through the landscape pursued from all sides by furious hunters, he's peppered with wounds and spattered with blood, and in his eyes you see horror and dread . . . that unicorn is really Christ, and for me, Dubenka, he is Andy Warhol too, he who was hit three times by Valerie Solanas, because she loved him even more than Liza Minelli did, I think Valerie loved Andy Warhol even more than his pop-star Debbie Harry did, and that's saying something . . . Of course, the one who loved Andy the most was his mum, that one-time folk artist, and he loved her too . . . Andy Warhol, saint, born in Pittsburgh, but whose parents came from Miková, over by Medzilaborce . . . Somewhere over there live the Ruthenians, and there a Jesus Christ could be born, distributing Coca-Cola to the believers and holy pictures multiplied by his silkscreening . . . That's my Andy Warhol, a man with the face of a released convict, a man with a wig of silvery grey, and his heart is a diamond larger than the Ritz, a man who died of heart failure, and was carried up to heaven in the cabin of Apollo 8 by a 4,000-tonne thrust Saturn 5 rocket, a pop-art heaven, and there he reigns to this day . . .

Dear Dubenka, these are words of mystification, but I can allow myself the luxury of canonising Andy Warhol, for that is the mystery of the moving metaphysical shooting gallery, the mystery of Puppenspiel, from which Goethe in the end with all his existence composed Faust . . . But in spirit I am still sitting in The White Horse, where the Lord's beloved Dylan Thomas sat and drank himself to death . . .

P. S. Dear Dubenka, here I sit back in Kersko, it's misty, the little cats are drenched and begging me to let them into the warm, but I'm a believer in the cold-water treatment, so out they sit in the shed in the hay and straw, like tiny little Jesuses. And I'm watching a broadcast from St Peter's, in Rome, where the Pope has just proclaimed the blessed Agnes a Saint, Agnes, who cared for the poor and founded a convent for the poor of Prague, in the spirit of Saint Francis, who was able to converse with the birds of the heavens, Agnes, who stands cast in metal on Wenceslas Square close to the right hand of Saint Wenceslas, where people lay flowers and hundreds of candles great and small . . . Saint Agnes, that Premyslid Princess of Prague . . . *Post*-Modern is simultaneously *Ost*-Modern . . .

Kersko, 10 November 1989
Translated by James Naughton

"A BOLD YOUNG QUARTERLY WHICH OFFERS A BERTH TO CHALLENGING NEW WRITING FROM EAST AND WEST."

THE TIMES

IN THE NEW EUROPE, STORM CHARTS THE LITERATURE OF POST-REVOLUTION. IN 1991, IT PUBLISHED WRITERS LIKE BOHUMIL HRABAL, PAWEL HUELLE, HERTA MULLER AND HANNA KRALL — MANY OF THEM MAJOR FIGURES ON THE CONTINENT APPEARING FOR THE FIRST TIME IN ENGLISH. BUT DON'T TAKE OUR WORD FOR IT.

Take Europe Buy STORM

STORM 4 IS OUT NOW WITH STORIES, EXTRACTS AND POETRY FROM • DRAGO STAMBUK • EWA KURYLUK • RICK MOODY • UNDINE GRUENTER • KATE STERNS • ADAM BODOR • URSZULA BENKA • GENEVIEVE SERREAU • NEW WRITING FROM EAST AND WEST • AVAILABLE FROM GOOD BOOKSHOPS • £5.00 • DISTRIBUTED BY JONATHAN CAPE ASSISTED BY THE ARTS COUNCIL OF GREAT BRITAIN AND GREATER LONDON ARTS